THE MAKING OF A **LEGEND**

IF IT DONT MAKE MONEY
IT DONT MAKE SENSE

THE MAKING OF A

LEGEND

**IF IT DONT MAKE MONEY
IT DONT MAKE SENSE**

SAMMYO

The Making of a legend© 2020
By Sammy O
Harlem's Own Sammy O LLC.

Printed in the United States of America

The Library of Congress has cataloged the soft cover edition as follows:
Sammy O

ISBN: 978-1-7923-3780-2

Artwork: www.HotBookCovers.com

Sales inquiries should be forwarded to:

Harlem's Own Sammy O LLC.
P.O. Box 855
New York, NY 10026

CONTENTS

ACKNOWLEDGEMENTS

I have to start by thanking the man above, my lord and savior Jesus Christ. Act 17:28 say's: "For in him we live and move and have our being" I wouldn't have or be nothing without GOD.

I have to thank my awesome wife, Monique. For everything, from reading and listening to early drafts, giving me advice on the project even in the middle of the night out of her sleep. Thank you so much. I love you.

Thank you to everyone on my team who helped me bring this project to life. Big Vic from 115th St thank you for keeping it real when it came to your wife's writing skills, you never lied when you told me that she was the real deal. Special thanks to my ever so patient, amazing writer Deborah "Sexy" Cardona who helped bring my stories to life and Dashawn Taylor, the greatest cover designer you can ever imagine.

Writing a book is not as easy as one may think but the end result is very rewarding. None of this would have been possible without the people who helped raised me, I'm eternally grateful to my Aunt/Mother Mary Brown (RIP) I truly have no idea where I would've been if she wouldn't have taken me.

To the mother of my children, thank you for your undeniable strength in both roles when I wasn't around to be the father you needed me to be.

To my children: Sammy O, Monay, Alicia, Tyriq, Shelby, Samson and Samara. If there was a do over button, I can press to be the father I am today I will press it without hesitation.

To my family:
My village of surrogate mothers Doris "Moody" Dixon (RIP) Gloria Richardson, Yvonne White, thank you for all you have done for my children and accepting them as your own grandkids.

My mother-in-law Selena who is always there for my family. I'm very and always grateful.
To my sisters from another mother Laurie and Brenda Goodwin, Gloria Thompson, Wendy Walcott –Bender, Andrea Hart and Sheila Dixon.

Thanks to Leon Mitchell.

ACKNOWLEDGEMENTS

To my nephew Wise thank you for your support you have always encouraged me to follow my dreams. You already know that I have always had your back and will continue to do so.

To my brother Kim Harrington and sister Regina Lucas thank you for everything you've done for me.

To the man who is never too busy for me to catch the special moments in my life, Thomas "Picture Man" Chubbs

To my 111th street crew, who taught me discipline, tough love, respect and so much more that helped me succeed in life **THANK YOU**: My cousin Ty Parker, Big Gary, Stinka aka Yah-Yah, Joe-Frog, Levi, Ike, brothers Norman, Kirk and Lawrence. Dwayne, Rick aka Ricky-Frog, and brother's Mark and Tootsie. Preston along with his brothers Draftin Aka Stink, Sellers Jr. Aka Boo, Vincent and niece Kim. Kurry, Franky, brothers Richard, Joe, the twins Buck-Wheat and Spanky and Ronnie and Johnnie, Jessy, brothers Darryl Junior Aka Fly, brothers Black aka Nate, Cliff aka Blue Steel, Miligan, Bucky, Bubby, Cuban-Mike, Clarence aka Hurk, DeWitt, DJ, Lenzie aka Pep, Wayne-O along with brothers Hoppo and Vernon, Scotty, Bear, Graveyard, Ray, Eric, brother Muzzo, Joe, George, Walley, Keith, Jessy Gray, Uncle Wille (RIP) Big Willie, Albee, Country, Charlie, Charlie Rock, House, Handsome, Wine, Barron, brother Dame, Russell, Kenny aka Pokey (RIP), Port, brothers Sterlin, Pookie-Doo and Boobie, Shelly, old man Jimmy, Spot and Smiley.

Finally, to those have been a part of my life's journey:

Spencer, T-Ferg, Bizz, Deuce (22), Baby Bob, Mike Booth, Tony Dread, Norega, Capone, Moe Blind, Black Rodney (139th) My brother in law Calvin, Shane "J.B", Wayne Davis, Ziggy, Guy Woods and the Woods family, Reggie (Storage), Party Rob, Achmir, Gerald "G-Rob" Robinson, Smoke Black, Quarter Field, Green Eye Red (RIP), Hot Rod, Big Nate, Skeeta (RIP), Big Al (117th) Patrick Hollinsworth, Slick (112th) Puerto Rican Johhny-O, 40 (Arie), Wise, Travis "YoungAceDeuce", Bunny and Dre Brown (114th St).

George "Cho-Cho" Smith
I will forever be grateful.

Finally, Free Darryl "D-Boss" Henderson,
Timothy "Timbo" Dixon,
William "Dougie Lime" Tucker and
Wayne "Wayneo" Green.

A big thanks to my buddy
Frankie P.
The Printer.

INTRODUCTION

HARLEM

A fabrication of the myth; Women were supposed to be seen and not heard until you met Beverly Harris a heroin addict who lived in her truth. The woman who exposed all of the aspects of the street life to me in the worst way. I Sammy O a nickname I was given by one of my street uncle's Cliff not because I liked to eat cheerios but because there was a time that there was nothing else to eat. The cheerios, cheese and peanut butter we received weekly were small contributions from the food pantry on 116th St. bet 7th and 8th avenue, contributions that were very much appreciated. Since being dropped off at my grandmother's house at the age of two then abruptly handed down to Aunt Mary I thought that those basic meals were something of the norm. There were many things in my world that seemed normal until it didn't.

In my world the women were engulfed in poverty, depression and addiction but most of all they were women with a voice that cut deep whenever need be.

Just like Beverly Harris my Aunt Mary was trapped in the world of addiction of alcoholism, with a bottle in one hand and a scrub brush in another Aunt Mary was the true definition of a woman and a mother. She did the best she could with what she knew. Especially when it came to a nappy headed kid who was not her own but hers, nevertheless. It didn't take long for me to realize that I wanted something more. Everything that Aunt Mary provided was appreciated but at an early age my curiosity came to life as I walked by a bar by the name Lorays located on 112th 7th Ave daily traveling back and forth from P.S.113.

Cecil's was another spot that many people from the neighborhood went into for various reasons like to play their numbers but mainly it was the spot for all the kids to get their penny candy and Let's not forget about Mikes grocery store. At Lorays I noticed all of the major players hanging out drinking eating or shooting pool. Being that they were not flashy brothers you would have never known that these men were deep into the dope game. Nor would you have ever known how dangerous they were until you crossed the line. Main rules to their way of thinking was never ever attempt to disrespect their block and the people who lived in it.

I use to notice a group of guys running back and forth providing a service and getting paid for it. I didn't know back then that that service or should I say the product they provided allow them the lifestyle so many in the hood craved. I noticed the hand to hand transactions monies being exchanged between them were in abundance. I noticed them dressed in the latest foot wear as I looked down at my feet to only find that the sneakers I wore would just have to do until Aunt Mary was able to bless me with a new pair. That desire to have the finer things in life became an obsession. Waiting for the next six months till I was able to get something new to wear seemed like an eternity.

So much so that when I thought about the things, I didn't have I thought about Beverly Harris and wondered if her addiction to heroin and the streets were more important than her son. No matter what her situation was I always hoped that she would come back to get me and give me everything that I desired as a child. But that would never happen, I knew that she had other plans and being a mother was not one of them.

I remember the day hope died.

"Your mother has been arrested for murder and she will be going to prison for a long time." Aunt Mary told me directly and without remorse then walked out of the room as though that type of shit wouldn't affect a kid. It did and that's when my life changed forever.

CHAPTER 1

MAMA LOVE

I can tell you a million stories about my mother, stories I have heard from family members and yeah sure those stories may have been true maybe exaggerated or just outright lies. I listened as everyone talked about her, me and how I ended up at Aunt Mary's house. I understood very little due to my age however, there is one story that I understood all to well and that is only because I lived it and I remember it all as though it was yesterday.

Summer of 1965, I remember my bones dislocating at the slightest touch. I remember the pain in my body as well as the pain I always felt in my stomach. It was a really disturbing time in my life to go hungry daily. I don't even know how I made it to the age of two but I did, guess that was God's plan. I remember my grandfather Big Sam walking into my mother's apartment looking at me and sweeping me off my feet. He carried me out the door, down the stairs and into his car. How he found me? I later found out that someone told him that Beverly was really doing badly and that she was not feeding me. They told him that she was taking the money and food stamps the government was giving her to use drugs. She was neglecting me in the worse way. That person had made it clear to Big Sam that if he didn't step in immediately, I was going to die. No child should ever have to endure such neglect this is why when I started having children, I made it a point to be there for them no matter what. I remember arriving at my grandmother Ruby's house. A lot of the things after that was unclear but what I do know is that my grandmother did not want the responsibly of taking care of a sick child. In her mind she felt that she was done with raising kids and she was not going to put that burden of a dying kid on herself, something she later regrets.

You see back in those days you either looked down on the street life or you accepted it. My grandmother didn't accept it, so she looked down on Beverly and the decisions she had made in life.

My mother was looked down on for many reasons the first one was because her first addiction was to sex. Beverly had fifteen kids, thirteen before me and another one after me. Like my grandmother explained before her passing she didn't respect a woman who continued to have children when all of her children were taken away from her for one reason or another. My brothers and sisters were spread out among Beverly's family and foster care. She claimed to not be nurturing so giving up her kids was no big deal to her. She moved on with her life as though they never existed. Then came me.

So, you see Beverly wasn't always a drug addict.

She became involved with my pops and that was when her addictions took a turn. How she became involved with drugs is still a mystery, all that is clear is that my pop was a hustler and Beverly use to steal his product to get high on the low. Pops knew something was going on but never really paid it any attention because like many others he was consumed by the streets. As her addiction worsen people noticed the change in her and would tell my pops but he was in denial. Respectfully, I could understand that no man wants to hear that their woman was using heroin or any drug. There was a sense of pride and there will always be a sense of pride in the men from Harlem.

Beverly started off by snorting the heroin she stole from my pops then eventually got introduced to shooting up by a family member by the name of Harold who was Aunt Mary's son.

Never understood back then why there wasn't a limit to this type of shit but once I hit the streets, things became clear. Drug addicts always and will always look for a way to get that next hit. So, if turning someone out gave them that, all values went out the window. The sad thing about that whole situation is that he recovered from his addiction, moved away and left Beverly out there. My pop was already locked up during that time, so she had no one. Upon her losing access to my pop stash Beverly hit the streets dragging me along with her.

And that was something my grandmother could not understand. It was already a tough situation for her, so she refused to raise me and that's when my Aunt Mary stepped up to the plate causing resentments between her son Harold and her decision to raise me. Although I forgave Harold trust me there were many people who I didn't.

CHAPTER 2

CHARLESTON SOUTH CAROLINA

At five years old I was forced to go down south, a trip that I dreaded. I was not trying to leave Aunt Mary's side, she was and will forever be the one who loved me unconditionally and she was the only mother I knew, so you can understand how a five year old would feel when being told that they was sending me to South Carolina for the entire summer.

She told me there was nothing for me to do in Harlem and the streets was not a safe place for me. She also told me about a program called the Fresh Air Fund that I could have gone to but because I was only five going on six, I wasn't able to go. The age range was from seven to eighteen years old. So, I had to wait another year to be eligible.

I cried screamed and even locked myself in the bathroom for what seemed like hours but according to Aunt Mary I was only in there twenty minutes. She told that story to anyone who would listen and then they would laugh about it.

Now that I look back on that day Aunt Mary had jokes about me.

Mainly because once I arrived to South Carolina I didn't want to come back to Harlem. I had the best time of my life and if you grew up in the south in that era you already know what I'm talking about. There weren't many kids from my neighborhood who got the chance to leave the city. However, those that did were blessed.

There were no restrictions in the south, well not at Grandma Viola's house anyway. She always treated me special and the love that she showed me was worth those trips all of the summers after that.

Grandma Viola wasn't really my grandmother she was my aunt, grandma Ruby's sister. But in her eyes, I was her grandson too. You know that saying "It takes a village to raise a child", well believe that because all of the women in my family raised me into the man I am today. They taught me to always treat women with respect, hold doors, pull out chairs, pick up the bill, and help with the bags but most importantly to speak in a tone where I could get my point across without being aggressive. Physical intimidation was unacceptable in our family.

The men had to be gentlemen, work hard, have integrity but most of all be a man of your word.

The females had to be ladies at all times no matter what they were going through. Prayer was an essential factor in my family. I can remember Viola always praying handing out the God bless you whenever she received you in her home and every time someone left.

Don't get me wrong we all grew up with values but there are two sides to every coin.

My first hands on experience at learning how to be a gentleman was when I played with my female cousins Wendy, Vivian, Marilyn and Jerry. Wendy who had become my best friend while my stay at Viola's was also learning, that how you present yourself to the world is how you will be treated.

The young women in my family were little ladies, respectful, good hearted they set goals and accomplished them, and they overcame obstacles and created a healthy lifestyle for themselves.

All families have their fair share of family members that get diverted from their upbringing and fall victims to the street life, but it doesn't mean that they were raised that way. Those that chose to go down that route made those choices on their own. Something like what happen to me.

Now when it came to me and my male cousin Jimmy, Violas only son well you already know our upbringing was a whole lot stricter. I always thanked God for all those lessons, little did I know that we were all being groomed to be productive members of society.

My choices in life had nothing to do with the way I was raised but like most who grew up in Harlem I became a product of my environment.

Going to South Carolina had been one of the best thing's Aunt Mary could have done for me, being there I learned how to ride a tricycle play outdoors without having to worry about the dangers that lurked on the streets of Harlem. I learned how to play with my cousin's share amongst each other, but the best thing for me was when I discovered the red wagon.

I couldn't get enough of it; this was one of my fondest memories and then when I found out that I could pump up the black handle and use it to steer myself around that was it for me.

I remember how every Sunday grandma Viola dressed me up in a black suit and not so shiny black shoes. I guess that's when my sense of style was born because I always had to add my own touch to the look by either spit shining my shoes or just wiping them down with a cloth and some water. She always told me that I cleaned up nice after we were done with the preparation. Her million dollar smile always made me feel good. I definitely looked forward to dressing up for church.

Sunday dinners were even better than what we ate during the week. Viola definitely did her thing in the kitchen, mac and cheese collard greens yams, sweet ham, roast pork, cornbread, peach cobbler and her special banana pudding, life was good in the south. When Viola found out from grandma Ruby what happened to me and how Beverly had almost starved me to death, she reinforced that I eat everything and anything I wanted. My cousins teased me about this all the time and still do.

Grandma Viola definitely was the one who opened up my appetite.

CHAPTER 3

POPS

That train ride felt like forever, I wasn't happy about going back to Harlem, there was nothing like waking up in the morning eating breakfast and hitting the outdoors. I knew that at home it would go back to staying stuck in the house staring out the window, only going outside when Aunt Mary had to run an errand or when a family member was going down to sit on the stoop. I was sad to leave Viola and my cousins yet excited at the same time. I missed Aunt Mary and I couldn't wait to see her, but I really couldn't wait to see my pops Sam Jr. Although I was too young to know why he had left in the first place I still was excited. Guess it was because I heard the excitement in everyone else. He had finally been released from prison and I couldn't wait to see him.

As the train pulled into my stop, I saw my uncle Homer there waiting for me. Homer was Aunt Mary's husband he was only related to me through marriage, but who said you had to be from the same blood line to be family. He was more family to me than most family members. Just like Aunt Mary, Homer stepped in to help raise me, he loved me like a son and because he didn't have children of his own his love, compassion, advice, and values were given to me. Homer was a hardworking man I used to watch him get up every morning no matter what to go to work. He always said there were no excuses no rain nor shine was going to stop him from being a responsible human being. If you didn't work, you couldn't pay the rent and if nothing else you had to pay your rent.

Watching him motivated me to do the same, school was a must in my house. Aunt Mary's famous line was "If my husband gets up every morning to go the work so will everyone else." No excuses that was just another value that was instilled in me. You wouldn't hear much from him during the week but when Fridays rolled around, I knew Uncle Homer was going to the liquor store to get a bottle of his favorite drink, hand me a dollar bill and then give Aunt Mary some money for the bills.

I looked forward to my allowance every week it was the only day of the week that I could go to Cecil's to buy some penny candy. By the time Uncle Homer could hand Aunt Mary her money I was out the door down the street and in Cecil's.

By the time I returned from the store I would find Homer already talking about the white man and how we couldn't trust them, didn't know if what he was saying were facts or if it was the liquor talking.

Either way it didn't matter he was the first man I looked up too.

My pop was my hero but Homer my teacher.

Uncle Homer grabbed my bag took my hand and walked me out of the Amtrak station and into the subway. As we rode the 2-train home we talked about my trip and how I looked good healthy and full of life. I'm telling you that was a big change since all people talked about was how skinny I was. How Aunt Mary had to feed me twenty-four hours a day to fatten me.

What a sight for sore eyes I saw Aunt Mary from a distance, and I started running towards her. I didn't realize how much I really did miss her until I jumped in her arms. She missed me to because while I was running to her she held her arms wide open for me to dive right in. That's that type of shit all kids long for.

After Aunt Mary held me for a second and let me go, I noticed my pops standing close by with a big smile on his face. So, I walked over to him, finally my hero was there in the flesh. I didn't have to hear any more stories about the man he was.

I was going to be able to find out for myself. But that thought quickly vision because while I was getting reacquainted with Sam Jr. I suddenly heard an argument coming from behind me, when we realized it was Aunt Mary who was yelling my pop pushed me to the side and confronted the man, they called J.C. he was the leader of the gang by the name of The Black Spades but that didn't stop my pop from handling his business.

I'm sure that J.C. felt threaten with everyone standing around confronting the situation cause why else would he take out a switch blade and cut my pop across the face.

That was the first time I had ever seen violence I didn't know how to take it all I can remember was that I was in a rage there was nothing I could do to protect my father. But I would never forget J.C. face and when time allowed, I was able to confront him. It was years later at my Aunt Gwendolyn Henderson funeral when I approached him.

"Do you remember me"?

He had the nerve to look at me as though I was an old friend, he was smiling asking me as well as himself "Where do I know you from"? I was so engrossed in the memory and in the fear that I felt when I was five years old that I wanted to see that same fear in his eyes.

After I told him who I was and what he had did to my father he tried to throw it off on another man who was part of his gang. When I was ready to take action, my family intervened telling me that this was not the place to execute any malicious intent.

I had to take a step back get my thoughts in orders and respect the fam, to see the fear in J.C. was not enough for me I wanted to lash out but I decided to fall back and leave it alone. He left shortly after and I never seen him again.

Now I know why the Italians had a strict rule for killing their rival's first son. It was their duty to make sure there were no cash outs, no returns, and no refunds.

CHAPTER 4

BEVERLY

As I got older, I realized that there was something missing in my life and that was my mother. I needed her, and as a young boy I longed for her, I had so many questions. I tried to keep those feelings to myself but whenever I got up the nerve to express that to my Aunt, I was reminded by her that my mother had abused, neglected and abandoned me. Because Aunt Mary was an alcoholic, she would go off on me every time she would start drinking. Whenever I would mention my mother, she would call my mother a junkie and say I was a junkie too.

Which was confusing to me because Aunt Mary always made sure I knew who my mother was. Upon her return to Harlem after losing her apartment in the Bronx Beverly roamed the streets looking for that next hit of dope. And since Harlem was known to have the best dope on the market, we all knew that she was in area.

When Aunt Mary began with the negative comments about my mother that shit bothered me. One day I took it upon myself to go see her at her usual hangout on 112th on 8th Ave in front of the liquor store. I started to look for my mother on a regular. I didn't care about what she was doing, all I knew was that she was my mother and that I loved her. It didn't matter either that she didn't want me or need me nor even miss me.

A part of me was always sad because of it, no matter what I did throughout my days I always felt empty.

When I got to the liquor store, I didn't see her I looked in the store, around the corner and up the block. She was nowhere to be found I asked a bunch of men who knew of her if they had seen her and they told me that she wasn't around, that she had left to go uptown. Later that evening Aunt Mary gave me the bad news.

I became eager to know what really happened and how she ended up in prison for murder. The story was that she had walked into a bar on 137th on Lenox Ave supposedly she asked a man at the bar if he was interested in buying something that she was selling. The man turned around and told her

"Does it look like I want to buy that? You fucking junkie bitch!"

She then stated "I may be a junky but I'm nobody's bitch." She then reached into her waistband and pulled out a twenty-five automatic.

"How you like this junkie now"!

The man looked at my mother and tried to stand up but before he could make a move Beverly shot and killed him.

I must have heard that story a hundred times, but I wanted to know the truth and I wanted to hear it directly from her. I also wanted to know why she never shared with me that she had gotten married to a man by the name of Norman Harris. I used to see him with her all the time but I didn't have a clue that he was my step-father.

When Beverly was arrested and sentenced to prison time at Bedford hills correctional facility for women. Norman, who was also on the streets decided to clean up his act. He admitted himself into a rehabilitation program called Day Top Village which was located on 40th St. between 5th and 6th Avenue in midtown. There is where he came to terms that he was not strong enough to kick his addiction on his own. Guess that is what happened to my mother while she was at Bedford cause when she was released, she never went back to the street. I believe that anyone who is trapped in an addiction is because they never had the chance to experience something different. It wasn't meant for Beverly to be junkie. I want to believe that she just got caught up.

Because of this I found it easy to forgive her.

Norman went through treatment by attending support groups learning the twelve steps of recovery and visiting my mother on a regular. He even started coming to 111th St. to come see me. I needed that at the time seeing him on his weekend passes made me feel closer to Beverly. I now wonder if seeing me made him feel the same way. I remember him picking me up and taking me to Day Top Village to spend the whole weekend with him. On one of those outings I told him that I wanted to see my mother, he tried to be compassionate as possible when he told me that she didn't want to see me. But I didn't take no for an answer, so he eventually took me.

Bedford hills was not a nice-looking place. There was something strange about the prison for sure. I noticed it right away as the bus from the metro north approached the prison. I stared out the window the whole entire time and even though it was warm out and the sun was shining, I noticed a grey cloud hovering over the prison. I tried to push my anxiety to the side because seeing Beverly was more important to me.

We were processed through, instructed to sit at a table where there was a partition separating the inmates from the visitors. We waited for her to walk in. When she did, she looked surprised, she walked over to Norman and I and sat down quietly. Our conversation started with her telling Norman "I told you not to bring anyone to see me because it makes my bid harder." Her tone was stern, yet I could tell that she was happy.

Norman told her that I wouldn't take no for an answer. So, he brought me to see her, not so much for her, but more so for me. He understood how I felt and he wanted nothing more than to reunion me with Beverly, and he did.

Beverly seemed at ease at this point. She then stated, "Yeah my son always looked for me." She became emotional as the visit went on.

Beverly also told us that she was embarrassed because they had pulled most of her teeth out due to her drug use and she didn't want anyone to see her that way. She tried to play it off by smiling with her mouth closed but to no avail. I noticed but I didn't care all I wanted was for her to see me, I mean really see me.

Although Beverly was caught up in the street life, she was a proud woman once she was able to get clean that pride shined in everything she did thereafter. A few missing teeth was not going to make me look at her differently I was living in the moment and I was happy.

Beverly had become a minister after being in prison for seven years, once she was released, she attended ministry school. And became a minister at the famous Canon Baptist church on 116th St. in Harlem. During her healing process my mother shared her truth with her congregation she became a walking testimony to the street life.

But most of all she became a lesson to me. Seeing Beverly out on the street as a kid forced me to align with my values. I vowed to never entertain the thought of ever indulging in drugs.

CHAPTER 5

THE BROTHERHOOD

It was 1976 when things began to change on 111th St. I was used to seeing the heroin addicts on the avenue but as time changed those same addicts started coming into the block to cop and sometimes even go into the buildings to get high. Where once the kids were protected of all that now we were being exposed to it. Because of it the older guys started taking notice and as a way to protect us from any outsiders they began to choose us as little brothers. The older guys were already out there running the streets. It wasn't important how they made their money and we as kids didn't ask any questions. All we cared about was getting whatever they gave us. Be it sneakers jeans and shirts, all hand me downs of course but still in good condition.

Is it safe to say that one man's trash was another man's treasure? Even when it didn't look like trash at all.

One thing about the older dudes they never disrespected us by giving us used items that looked like used items. They wanted us to look good and besides they were making too much money to do something like that.

I was lucky enough to have two street brothers that looked out for me, the first one being Cliff. He had not only adopted me as his little street bro he actually acted and treated me like one.

One day after school I was walking down the block towards my building. Cliff was standing there, I guess waiting for me, and he seemed preoccupied looking back and forth as though trying to avoid someone or something. When he saw me, he called me out to hurry up and get in the building. He entered the building before me and I quickly followed. When I approached him, he asked me to open my bookbag he then went in his jock strap and pulled out fifty quarters of heroin and told me to hold that package for him. Who was I to question it? I had to look out for him the same way he had always looked out for me. I didn't think twice about it. I closed the bag ran up the stairs and into Aunt Mary's house and stashed in under my mattress. Three days later Cliff came back to get it. He asked me if I still had his work. When I told him yes, he didn't look surprise, he went on the tell me that the cops were chasing him that day and that's why he had to get rid of the work and lay low for a few days. I had made it my business to make sure that his product was secure. Although Cliff never told me when he would be back for it. I knew that eventually he would and like I was taught by the old O.G's I had to be a stand-up nigga. Loyal to those who were loyal to me. He knew who he was dealing with, he knew that he could trust me to handle the situation and I did.

I gave Cliff the bag and told him to keep it. He looked at me dug into his pocket and gave me my first hundred-dollar bill. I couldn't believe it and again I didn't ask no questions. I thanked him for the money and he thanked me for being loyal. On that day I learned that being loyal was the number one code in the streets.

Another lesson that I learned while growing up on 111th St. was to never leave one of your brothers alone, if you go anywhere together you come back together. A lesson I learned the hard way.

One day my friend Eric and I was walking on 110th St. on Central Park West Eric had a bike and from nowhere a group of guys jumped out at him and tried to take it. Eric refused to give it up, so he started fighting with them. I called myself trying to get help, so I ran to 111th St. which was right around the corner. I yelled down the block that Eric was being jumped and the whole block stood at attention. Cliff and some of the others ran towards Eric and chased them away. But that incident didn't end there. When I thought I was doing the right thing by getting help I had gotten my ass whopped for leaving him alone in the first place. I didn't know that I was putting Eric in a dangerous situation and I also didn't know that on that day I would learn a valuable lesson.

Cliff was definitely my big brother he always made sure that I had a few dollars in my pocket and that my stomach was full.

Looking back now that is how we met I was sitting at the counter at Lorays eating a lettuce and tomato sandwich because that was all I could afford at the time. He walked in looked at me for a few seconds. He then placed an order with the bartender old man Melvin. He instructed him to give me a plate of rice, lima beans and a steak. Yep, he ordered my very first steak and from that day forward Cliff had become my brother for life. Not because of the food although I appreciated it from the heart but because since that day, he took care of me never once asking me for anything in return.

Cliff was about ten years older than me so I could never really hang out with him and his circle so I started hanging around my cousin Ty. Who is more like a brother than a cousin.

Ty was eighteen a little closer to my age of thirteen years old he was a wise and charismatic young man, a ladies' man, he was light skin, dressed fly and was already making a name for himself.

Because of his personality and his sense of fashion people in the neighborhood started calling him fly Ty.

And without a doubt I grew to admire him.

He had a lot of beautiful women coming through the block to see him, each one prettier than the other. At thirteen years old I was already fantasizing about being with girls, a little late for my age if you ask me because some of the other kids were already sneaking off to central park to make out and get there feel on.

I had growing pains and as I watched Ty in the moment with all these beautiful girls, I became curious.

I made it my business to be around him and he made it his business to know my every move, I had become his prodigy. Don't know if he ever knew this but I was like a sponge, I picked up on everything he did.

Our conversations were deep and still to this day we maintain the same vibe. Just like in the old days we still call each other to reminisce about the good old days.

The brotherhood is solid.

We talked about everything life the streets females etc. One day he asked me if I had ever been with a girl before

34

and I told him no. He had a few jokes about it but I didn't pay him any mind. I changed the subject because at thirteen I was very shy, I was still not where I wanted to be in the looks department, and again I was teased a lot by the other kids in my neighborhood.

I was still nappy headed still didn't dress the way most of the other kids dressed. Basically, I was uncomfortable in my own skin. Ty always told me not to worry about that that there was more to life then my appearance. I tried to believe that but I had all these bumps on my face and to add insult to injury I had to wear Coca-Cola glasses with tape on the side to hold them together.

I knew then and I know now that he was just protecting me emotionally.

Several weeks later while we were hanging out on the stoop. I remember a local prostitute walking down the block, Ty called her over and told her that he would pay her to take care of me and Eric's older brother Muzzo. I was not trying to go there but Ty took us upstairs to an apartment in an abandon building that we took over and made it our own. The chick went straight to the bedroom and undressed. I refused to go into that room behind her, I had made a whole bunch of excuses but Ty wasn't having it, he forced me into the room and told me to handle by business. I came out of that room several minutes later with my chest sticking out. Little did Ty know that he had a created a monster.

Pussy had become an addiction and I would do anything to get it. But what I wanted more than anything else in the world was to change my appearance because with good looks and money, it was easy to get the women.

I was so desperate that I went as far as to listen to my cousin Wayne-O when he told me that the only way to clear up my face from all those bumps was to spread a female's pussy juice all over my face. I hung on to his every word due to me wanting to enhance my looks.

One day while hanging out in the apartment he told me to go into the bedroom where he had his girl laying up, he told her to the spread her legs then he turned to tell me to whip my hand across her pussy then rub it all over my face. Wayne-O guaranteed me that it would clear up my face. I became so self-conscious over those bumps that I did that dumb shit and Wayne-O couldn't stop laughing. It didn't work and I felt so stupid for listening to him. I was so naïve.

These were the sick type of motherfuckers I grew up with on 111th St. even though I had many friends and family on the block, Cliff and Ty were the ones who had molded me into the man I am today. I learned so much from them. Cliff valued me as a human being dropping jewels on a regular like a father and Ty was more like my crimey. He took me under his wing and exposed me to many things, good or bad. Each encounter became a lesson, there wasn't anything that we would experience that didn't have a message behind it.

Ty always had his ear to the street making his transitions from one scenario to another always smooth. His demeanor that of a real one is why Ty was welcomed into any establishment. There was an after hour by the name Fagazie's between 117th St. and 118th St. On Lenox Avenue that Ty would go to gamble. One night he asked me to come with him it was late at night and he didn't want to leave me alone on the block. Once in there I recognized a few of the major players from Harlem sitting around a table. They were some heavy hitters I knew this because I kept my ear to street too. There wasn't anything that Ty knew that I didn't know as well. It wasn't intentional it just worked out that way.

Ty put his money on the table in front of him the houseman passed him the dice. He had to beat the bank man's number. I don't really remember if Ty won but what I do remember is when it was my turn to roll the dice there was a gentleman with his hand on the table. I asked him to move his hand because I didn't want the dice to hit him. Ty quickly intervene by telling me to chill, I ignored him and told the gentleman to move his hand again. Ty again intervene this time telling the man to pardon me because I didn't mean no disrespect, come to find out that that man was Nicky Barnes. I lost one hundred dollars on that play I was complaining that it was due to Nicky's hand being in the way guess because I was a younger brother, he offered to give me the money back. Ty dumb said no we good and left.

Ty and I headed back towards the block the sun was coming up when a dude name D.J. came up to me as I sat in front of my building accusing me of stealing his package from the basement. Ty was already pissed off about game that made him go wild on D.J. he defended me when he realized that D.J. was trying herb me. It didn't take much for Ty to transform when it came to me. That when I realized that D.J.'s bark was bigger than his bite.

I was learning how to finesse the streets the game and the women. How to create a long-lasting impression was key. I would say and do things I thought would get me noticed there was another situation I got myself caught up in but this time Ty wasn't around.

There was a dude by the name of Pete who was walking up from the Ave with his girl. As they passed by, I yelled out

"Yo! When you get tired of that lame come get some of this."

The words came out of my mouth so fast that I couldn't take it back. I thought I was being funny, but I think I was really testing the waters.

Before I knew it, Pete tried to bum rush me, I got up from where I was sitting and started running. But he caught up to me and smashed a bottle into my face. Blood dripped from the side of my eye and till this day I still have a scar. That scar will always remind me to never be disrespectful towards another man's woman. I was far from a dummy I only had to go through these unfortunate situations once. It didn't take much for me to pick up on things the first time around. I have seen many dudes come into certain situations, get themselves out of it then turn around and do it all over again.

Common sense isn't actually common from person to person in my opinion.

All of the things I was experiencing were things I had to go through in order to understand the challenges I was about to face in life.

There were cardinal rules to this shit and the rules don't change but the people do.

I started to change, but the values that were instilled in me didn't, I knew right from wrong but when you are surrounded by people who were always in survival mode you tend to start looking at life in the same way. The more I saw how people moved in their everyday activities, I realized that selling drugs had become the fastest way to get out of the hood.

I needed to do the same. I was tired of looking like a bum, I was tired of being hungry all the time, I was tired of everyone else looking out for me. I had to come up with a way to take care of myself.

The block loved me but it also tortured me on a daily, and I was tired of that shit. Some jokes just weren't funny anymore, so I came up with a plan.

CHAPTER 6

THE GAME

The plan was to save up all of the money that Cliff and Ty gave me and then head out to the Bronx in hopes of doubling my money. I come from a long line of gamblers father, uncles' cousins who all found a way to hustle without the hustle. My game of choice was Pitty Pat which is an international card game mainly played at casinos or the underground gambling joints However, in the hood I played this game at my families famous rent parties.

Rent parties are parties people had in the hood when it was time to pay the rent and they were short or didn't have the money at all.

The house {apartment owner} would charge a fee for every hand that was dealt at their tables. The set up was simple three, four maybe five tables with up to five players at each table. Each hand that was dealt at a table the house would get paid. Making them a small killing at the end of the night. Some of these parties sold food, alcohol and played music anything to get people in there to spend their money at the table.

Pitty pat is a pretty easy game to play all you need is a standard deck of cards, money and luck.

Though it may not be apparent at first, the objective is to make three pairs starting from a five-card hand.

Once I would get my money up, I would go over to my family house in the Bronx and play; on a good night I would win but when I lost I lost, my cousins Timbo, D-Boss and I came up with another way to make some quick cash when the card games went sour.

Yankees stadium was just up the block and when there was a baseball game there would be thousands of people attending. My cousins wandered around the stadium at first to just have something to do then we came up with a plan to get money while we were there.

We watched how the white folks flaunt their money as freely as they bought food at the concession stands and bought souvenirs at the souvenir stands. It was as though they were provoking us into being envious of them. And to be honest we were envious therefore we had decided to start snatching their money right out of their hands and running away as though we had won the lottery.

It's crazy how I went from being a shy little kid, to gambling, to snatching money from the white folks at Yankee stadium.

I became cocky with it because I was fast and I knew they weren't going to catch me, and once I made it down the block onto Gerard Avenue I was gone.

We used to also take the 2 train and go downtown to the diners and steal the tips that customers would leave at the table for the waitresses. We did these things to survive not because it was a game to us but because we needed to eat. We were in survival mode all the times; not one day would pass by that we weren't scheming. It was sad that a bunch of kids had to steal just to get the basic necessities but there was no time to think about that, we just did what we had to do to get by. I remember looking for a spot in Harlem where we could get something to eat at affordable prices. Sherman's became the most economical.

At Sherman's on 145th & 146th on 7th Avenue we were able to get spaghetti's ribs and potato salad for only five dollars a plate, so we went there damn near every night.

If we were in the Bronx, we would go to crown donuts on 161st.

One-night D-Boss came up with the bright idea of breaking into a warehouse on 149th we were walking across the bridge from 145th and he told us to break into a paint factor to get spray paint so that we could tag the trains. We never broke into a private property to steal anything but there was a first time for everything. We didn't need to do that, but we tried to do it anyway.

As we walked up to the warehouse, we had it all mapped out. I would be the one to climb up to the roof open the roof door get inside and then open the front door for them. I must have triggered a silent alarm because before I was able to get inside a police officer came around the property parked his car and saw me on the roof. Next thing I knew they had shined their flashlights in my direction. I looked over the edge of the building, I saw Timbo still standing by the main door waiting for me but when I looked around for D. Boss he was nowhere to be found.

The officers yelled up at me to come down, when they noticed that I wasn't moving fast enough they yelled up at me again. "That if I didn't come down immediately, they would be coming up to get me."

You would think that I would have listened the first time they spoke to me or that I would be scared at the thought of being caught. But I wasn't I found it funny because to me we were having fun.

I eventually complied and came down. Once I hit the pavement, they immediately put me and Timbo in handcuffs. Timbo knew that D-Boss was under a car hiding so as we were being escorted towards the police vehicle he yells out.

"D-Boss come on out we are caught."

He was about ten years old, so he didn't have a clue that he was snitching.

Once we arrived at the police station, they called all of our parents my Aunt Christine Dickson came to pick up Timbo and my Aunt Gwendolyn Henderson came to pick up D-Boss.

But when they called Aunt Mary, he said she wasn't picking up no one as a matter a fact she said "If you got him keep him."

I couldn't believe that Aunt Mary would leave me there that shit hurt me. Both of my cousins went home and I sat at the precinct awaiting their next move.

While I sat there, I thought about Aunt Mary and how I felt about her, I couldn't understand how she could have turned her back on me. There had to be a logical explanation. It was either she didn't want or love me anymore or she must had been drinking. Either way I felt abandoned an emotion I always dealt with while growing up thanks to Beverly.

The cops didn't know what they were going to do with me, according to the higher up I had to be taken to family court and family court then sent me to Spofford.

Spofford was a juvenile detention center located in the Hunts Point area of the Bronx. I had heard rumors of the place and to know that I was on my way there made me uneasy. Spafford, once infamous for both detainee abuse and poor living conditions made me think about all the things I complained about. Even though I thought I had it bad I sure as hell didn't want to get into something worst.

Suddenly gratitude came into play as the van courtesy of children services pulled up to an old dirty building.

There was what we call a bubble with an officer inside he asked for paperwork he read through it then suddenly the gates rolled open and I was be escorted into the building.

I went through intake I was given a uniform and then assigned a housing unit and a cell. A part of me was in shock for the most part. However, I knew I had to snap out of   it quickly or I would be one of those juvies who the others would fuck with.

"Chow call!" an officer yelled as all the inmates started to line up. I followed suit ran through the drill like nothing, once in the mess hall I noticed a door, open towards the side of the kitchen. I don't know what I was thinking at the time but instead of getting in line to get a tray I walked towards the door walked out found a path that lead to the street. I hailed down a cab and went straight to 111th St.

God was on my side that day because when I arrived to 111th St. Cliff and Ty was in the block. They saw me get out the cab they paid for it and of course they started with the jokes. Those jokes were welcoming at that point and with good reason, I still had on the prison uniform.

CHAPTER 7

BLACK OUT

S ummer of 1977 on July 18th New York City underwent an electrical outage which affected most of my neighborhood. It was as though lighting struck over Harlem and the whole city went black.

It was still early in the evening before it happened and the block was filled with our families hanging out on the stoops listening to music from their boom-boxes, As some of the kids ran up and down the street playing stick ball, sewer to sewer football and skullies, while the others played by the fire hydrants with plastic buckets and tin cans with cut outs that created a homemade cannon. It was about ninety degrees; no breeze and the sidewalks were scorching hot. You could see fans from the windows nearby spinning slowly yet there was no relief from the heat that engulf the city.

During the summers we would open the fire hydrants with a big wrench daily to create our very own water park.

It was already getting late and the sun had gone down and all of the streetlights were coming to life. The water from the hydrant streamed down the side of the curb and onto the avenue where everyone who passed by took comfort as the cool water touched their feet including mine. I was having a good day hanging out with my friends but a part of me wanted to get away. This particular summer I didn't go down south I had to stay in Harlem. Aunt Mary called herself punishing me for my little breaking and entering episode. Since, break out from Spofford Mary realized that she was losing control over me.

There really wasn't anything to control though I just did what I had to do to get what I needed; she wasn't in a position to get me my basic needs so I had to do whatever it took to feel half way normal.

I don't quite remember what I was doing at that moment when all the lights went out. But I do remember that 111th St. had plunged into complete darkness. I heard people screaming on the streets, down the block and out the windows. People were coming out of their apartments spilling out onto the street drenched in sweat yelling out that the electricity had gone out.

No one knew all the facts; all we knew was that there was a blackout. According to the data provided by Con Ed the power outage was caused by stress on the system due to a series of lightning storms in Westchester County. It was a dark day in more ways than one, stress to the system okay, but what about the stress that the people of Harlem went through?

People started running into my block screaming saying that everyone was going crazy and that they were breaking into the local businesses to steal.

I saw people running past me with T.V.'s furniture clothes and shopping carts full of food. I had never experienced anything so crazy in all my life. Harlem was in a uproar and the crazy thing is that I wanted to get in, helping Aunt Mary was the first thing I thought of as I started running towards 116th but by the time I got there all of the windows of the store fronts were shattered, people were already inside grabbing merchandise. It was crazy and to make matters worse the thieves were robbing thieves and like the old saying goes there is no honor among thieves.

Even the hustlers got in on it they were sticking up the dope friends who came to them in hopes of selling them their stolen goods, no one was safe it was every man for them self-situation. I was following the crowd walking back towards 111th St. trying to get my hands on something to bring home like everyone else. When I noticed that Mike's grocery store was wide open, I immediately ran into the store grabbed some garage bags and got to work. I went straight to the meat department there were so many people grabbing the packs of meat while shoving others out the way. There were some people helping each other out talking about let's get all this and split it later. I didn't pay them no mind I remained focused taking whatever I could get my hands on.

I was able to get a bag full of meats then I ran up the aisle and threw some can goods in the bags. I struggled out that store. I could see myself now trying to get down the block dragging two garage bags behind me. I was a skinny kid, and those bags were heavy. By the time I got in front of my building. I only had one of the bags the other bag ripped causing all of the food to spill onto to the sidewalk, so I had to leave it behind. It took all of me to carry that one bag up the stairs and into Aunt

Mary's house only to be cursed out and told that she didn't want that shit in her house.

I tell you Aunt Mary was something else after all I went through to get her those items to only refuse them.

Upset about it, I dragged the bag out into the hallway knocked on our neighbor's door Ms. Shirley Preston's mother and I gave it all to her. At least they were appreciative of the small gesture. Till this day I don't know why Aunt Mary didn't want that food, in my eyes I thought I was doing some good for the family. In her eyes it was only a matter of time that I would get myself caught up in a situation I wouldn't be able to get myself out of, or it could have been that Homer was all in her ear about me.

Homer was a law a bidding citizen for real.

There were no cutting corners when it came to him. Although he stayed behind the scenes, he did make it a point to express his dislike of my behavior to my aunt.

I went back downstairs I walked to the corner in front of building 200 and witnessed my first homicide.

Two guys were arguing about a stolen T.V. one wanted to sell it and the other refused. I could hear them going back and forth with each other, then out of nowhere I heard a gunshot. When I looked in their direction all I seen was one of them dropping to the ground. Blood poured out of him so fast he died right there on the street. While the rest of the city was turmoil.

There was never a dull moment in Harlem.

CHAPTER 8

THE HUSTLE

The years were passing by quickly and with each passing day I couldn't stand to stay in the same situation. I continued to steal to survive but as I got older the risk of getting caught was higher. I stayed around the neighborhood in hopes of catching a break, but until then I had to roll with the punches.

The drug game was becoming more and more transparent. Now that heroin had become a household name, we had seen more and more white people coming to Harlem to cop. I remember seeing them starting off as stop and go addicts until they were becoming cop and stay addicts.

When the weekend rolled around and those luxury cars with Connecticut and Jersey plates pulled up, we already knew that it was going to be a major pay day. I wasn't in the game yet because no one would give me a break. Cliff had a lot to do with that he had made it a point to let everyone who was hustling on the block to not turn me out to the streets. However, I soaked up the scene observing their every move.

I played scenarios out in my head as I watched from a distance, from how they pulled up, parked their cars and went into the building where Ty was already posted up and ready to serve.

These out of town niggas came right there was no half stepping with them their money was long and the product was even longer. The street value of a quarter in Harlem was fifty dollars but Ty sold it to the out of towners for seventy dollars. These white boys would come to get anywhere from one hundred to two hundred quarters at a time, a street value of fourteen dollars a pop so they couldn't afford to run out and if they did, the block would look out for the block. Each building had their own crew and although everyone had something different to offer, they all looked out for each other by giving up their product to seal the deal. This was a time that there was enough for everyone to eat, not like in the nineties when the hustler became territorial.

Then there was the out of towners that came through to pick up weight. It didn't matter what they sold it for in their hometown as long as they came to Harlem correct.

Nate the main supplier to his crew and Ty who was his lieutenant made at least twenty thousand dollars on a Friday night in profit. They had their runners out there all-night hustling for them. I was supposed to be in the house by eleven pm, but I was so mesmerized by the lifestyle I never made it home on time.

Tired and hungry from standing around as the block got paid, I would sneak into Aunt Mary's house at the break of dawn. My cousin Sheila who was more like a sister, she was also living with Aunt Mary. Sheila came to live with us when her mother became a heroin addict and couldn't take care of her. That was one thing about my aunt she never allowed anyone of the kids in our family to go into the system, so she was raised too. Sheila always had my back, no matter what time it was I would tap on the front door where she slept by, she would run to the back of the house and open the window for me. I would sneak in quickly and go to sleep. In the morning when Aunt Mary would find me sleeping in the house she would go off on Sheila because she knew it was her who was letting me in. Mary hammered the window shut with some nails leaving me out the street to fend for myself. It got so bad that Sheila was being threatened to be thrown out the house because of me.

On the nights I didn't make it in the house by eleven pm. I would head downtown to the all-night movie theater on 42nd St. to sleep. I would go downtown a lot, until one-night Ms. Betty told me to go upstairs to her house to get some rest. Ms. Betty is Nate mother and one of Sam Jr's side pieces at the time she was a blessing to me in so many ways. Another one of the women who looked out for me while growing up. That somehow turned out to be the story of my life It was always a woman who put me on my feet who secured the investment, ME.

Ms. Betty was a wild one she use to curse everyone out and if u dared answer her back, she would pull down her pants in the middle of the street and tell you to kiss her ass. Aunt Mary followed suit and started doing the same shit. They had become partners in crime.

I started going to Ms. Betty house a lot, one because my father was always up there and two because she never gave me a hard time, she was already experiencing the ins and outs and the late-night knocks on the door due to Nate who was out on the block hustling 24/7. So, it didn't bother her that I would come over to her house late.

I had become very sick one day after eating Arthur Treachers fish and chip. I had decided to go up to Ms. Betty house to lay down for a while, I went into the back room and slept on and off for about two days with high fever and very little to eat because I couldn't hold anything down not even water.

Ms. Betty and her daughter- in-law Wendy Nate's girl checked on me, but their diagnosis was the flu. And what did I know I trusted that they knew what they were talking about, so I just kept on sleeping.

On the third day I was feeling weak and disorientated, I was able to somehow get up and walk into the living room where I found Nate, Ty and one of Nate's runners, Pepsi. I didn't have the chance to go into the bathroom and look at myself yet when Pepsi stated "Yo! What the hell is wrong with your eyes?"

I remember saying "What, what's wrong?", and then I ran into the bathroom to see that my eyes were yellow! I was rushed to the hospital where they took my blood, started me on an I.V. drip and isolated me in a private room.

When the results came back, I was told that I was lucky to have gone to the hospital when I did. I was diagnosed with Hepatitis A and it was already causing Jaundice which is yellowing of the eyes. The doctor's recommendation was to get plenty of rest eat right and drink lots of water. So much for the medical service in Joint Disease Hospital. Thank God that Wendy had suggested that I go to the emergency room I jumped into a cab and I made it there just in time, if it wasn't for her, I would have been dead. I was admitted for about three days, when I returned to the house, I found out that Nate had beat her ass for that.

I was such a loyal individual and I felt that I owed Wendy my life that somehow her grief became my grief making us very close friends.

CHAPTER 9

DOMESTIC VIOLENCE

Domestic Violence came in many forms physically, mentally, and verbally. The first time I experienced anyone being abused was when my father hit one of his women in front of me. He was not one of those men who knew how to express himself through words due to lack of education. Which made him feel very insecure. The women that Sam Jr. would get involved with were women of substance educated, hardworking and loyal first to themselves and then to him. But he couldn't see that about them. This particular woman seemed weak, she allowed him to dominate her every move then there were others that were strong enough to walk away from him and, did.

He was an abuser he knew how to get a woman, but he didn't know how to keep them. It was a disgusting display of a small-minded man living in a grown man's world. Clearly at that time I thought that that's how it was supposed to be, so I eventually started to do the same when I got older.

I too become aggressive towards women; it wasn't personal it was just my way of having control of a situation whenever one arose. My hands became bi-sexual it didn't matter what sex you were. If you violated, you got violated. As I started to surround myself around knowledgeable men, I began to learn that striking women was a sign of weakness. I never wanted to portray myself in that way. Because when you know better you do better.

The second time I experienced domestic violence was at Ms. Betty's house. Once I found out that Nate had hit Wendy for helping me, I started to be more aware that he would abuse her all the time, even before I came into the picture.

Nate was another one of those brothers who was insecure his anger ran deep. It all started when Ms. Betty treated him differently from his other siblings. He had a sister and a brother who were both light skin. Nate was the only dark one in the family and Ms. Betty always reminded him that they didn't have the same father. Ms. Betty was verbally abusive towards him something that affected him throughout his childhood. He began to abuse Wendy in hopes of holding on to the one thing he had control over. He manipulated her into believing that he loved her he would belittle her and then make it seem as though he didn't mean to do it. Ask for forgiveness only to do it all over again.

Wendy grew up in Esplanade garden in a loving home with her mother and grandmother although her family had their struggles, she had never experienced such violence. She just didn't come from that lifestyle.

When she started dating Nate while in High School everything was great until she started to find out that he had multiple girls throughout the neighborhood. When she confronted him, he would become angry argue with her and tell her to go to his house and stay there. That became the new normal for her so much that he made her quit school while he continued to go to SUNY College at old Westbury and sell drugs on the block.

Nate might had been insecure and jealous, but he was also very smart and charismatic. He seduced his way into Wendy's life making her feel that with each black eye he was showing his love. As the beatings progressed so did my awareness to what was going on with her.

She would stay in his room afraid to do anything outside of what he told her to do. She had become depressed and withdrawn from her family not being able to see them for weeks due to the bruises she had on her face.

Not only did he cheat and beat on her he would play this sick game where he would intertwine his relationship with her with the one, he had on the street.

There were times that he would have his runners out on the block hustling all week and when it was time to get paid, he would tell his runners that someone stole the money. Then turn around and blame Wendy. He made it to that he would beat Wendy in order to make it believable to his crew.

I hated that she was becoming immune to that type of treatment, but I couldn't do anything about it. All I could have done was become some type of comfort for her.

She started to talk to me about what she was going through with Nate and I was able to vent about what I was going through with Aunt Mary. I started to stay over a lot more because Aunt Mary made my life impossible her drinking had gotten so out of control; she too had become abusive. And to make matters worse she and Ms. Betty began to experiment with angel dust.

Wendy and I would play cards talk about our personal issues then turn around and find a way to laugh about silly things that went on in the block.

She was a few years older than me but we vibed. I was only about fifteen years old when we became good friends. Guess we both needed someone who could understand our grief without judgement. That friendship has lasted a lifetime and although we eventually went in different directions, I was blessed to find her after being arrested and going to prison, we picked up where we left off.

CHAPTER 10

WOLF OR SHEEP

G oing in another direction was an understatement, my life was about to get serious. As I continued to observe the street life, I wanted nothing more than to get on. I had the formula to success already mapped out in my head, all I needed was someone to give me that opportunity. I was pissed off that the brotherhood of 111th St. kept seeing me as a little dude that they needed to protect. I had outgrown all that bullshit I was not going to continue to stand around watching them play ball. Every day I would sit on the sidelines yelling out to whoever would listen.

"Coach put me in I can play. Yo! Coach take me off the bench!"

Coach being the boss, Play being the drug game.

I knew that the more runners you had the more money you can make. I yelled out that statement every day until it finally happened.

My break had come in the form of Hart he saw me on a daily basis waiting for my turn patiently. He called me out one day and asked me if I thought I was ready? When I told him I had been ready, he handed me a package. What the fuck he do that for? it was on after that! I walked up to home plate grabbed that bat (package) and got to swinging. For about a week I had proven myself to be reliable and worthy of the spot he had given me.

He had given me my first package of twenty-five quarters of heroin and twenty-five half a quarter. I stood in the lobby of 215 of my building the same building where Aunt Mary lived in. It had gotten to the point where surviving superseded her opinion or anyone's opinion for that matter. I was never one to blame others for my circumstance, but I sure as hell was going to be the one to change it.

For about a week I was on my A game we had a system that got us through the days without no arrest no robberies no violence. I would stand in the lobby serving the customers while Hart steered them in my direction. When I said that I had already mapped out my road to success I meant it. First and foremost, I had to make sure that I wasn't caught slipping, the first thing I did which was necessary was that I rigged my building. There was no way that I was going to get caught out there by the police if I could avoid it. The second thing I did was get familiar with the 25 automatic Hart had given me. Many had made the mistake of stashing their guns under trash cans or on top of a tire of a parked car. I kept that gun on me at all times set and ready to shoot.

What was the point of stashing your weapon nearby if you didn't have a chance in hell to get to it if danger came your way? I'd rather catch an eight-month bid on a gun charge then get killed. I may had been young, but I was slick beyond my years. That first week I made more money that I had ever seen in my life. Yeah, I saw the others making money, but I was never one to count other people's paper. I stayed focused on my own situation. I was doing good, made a few thousand dollars had the building secure and Hart was impressed with me and how I moved.

I thought I had everything covered until Cliff. When he saw what was going on, he put a stop to it with just a few words. He was so pissed off that Hart turned me out to the game that he threatens him and told him to never give me work again.

Little did he know that I was already turned out way before Hart came along, I had learned the business from him. But it goes to show you the undeniable power he possessed on the block.

It's sad that a few years down the road Cliff had lost his woman his wealth and his mind. When Cliff caught a short bid on the island for a gun charge his woman started fuckin his connect, I don't want to say that he was weak minded over a woman. But when you love and I mean really love someone, a betrayal to that magnitude can cause the unspeakable. After doing his bid things were not the same his woman was gone, he started smoking dust which caused him to give up on life. That's when he became homeless.

Once I was put back on the side lines, Cliff still looked out for me. And that was all good but again I wanted to be my own man. I had so much respect for him that I basically fell back and found other things to do where I was still in the game without being in the game. Whenever the block came across some new product, I was the one who ran around the neighborhood looking for Claw. If anyone remembers Claw you know that he wasn't a very desirable looking man. He was strung out on drugs had a swollen hand the size cantaloupe with abscess all over it and his fingernails so long and thick they looked like claws.

That is how he got his name. Although he looked that way, he was the most reliable dope fiend in the hood, if the new product got his stamp of approval the product would be put out for circulation.

Buckwheat and Spanky the twin brothers who I grew up under on 111th St. were also out on the block slinging dope. Once Claw gave the okay on the new product our block was flooded. Lines of dope fiends ran up the block and around the corner.

Buckwheat had his way of doing his thing just like the others, even though I wasn't serving any more, I made sure to look out for those that were. One-night Buckwheat was out there alone serving some people when I noticed that he was being robbed. I walked up on building 203 when I saw two unfamiliar face. I noticed that they had a gun on him and also noticed that he was trying to talk his way out of it. I slowly backed up and went into the basement and grabbed my gun. When I headed back upstairs the dudes were running out the building towards the avenue. I immediately followed suit raised my arm and started to shoot. They ran across 7th Ave and jumped in a car, but I was on their asses they were unable to pull off due to me reaching the passenger window and letting off a few shoots until I ran out of bullets. Don't know if I shoot the driver because he pulled off.

WOLF OR SHEEP

I went back up the block looking for Buckwheat, fool was standing in front of the building looking shook. Before he was able to say a word, I told him to give me some bullets.

He had the nerve to tell me that he needed his bullets and didn't have any bullets to give away.

How the fuck can someone say some dumb shit like that.

Can't give me no bullets when I just saved his ass from being killed.

It wasn't about Buckwheat quote unquote. It was about them violating the block and I had to a send message.

Once I bust my gun that night the block looked at me different. We all have a part to play in protecting our own. We threw up our hands, we shot guns, we stomped people out we even went as far as getting Spanky and his dogs.

No one was allowed to come from another block to hustle on 111th St. that was law.

Spanky walked into the block one day and saw a guy standing in front of 215 selling dope he came up to him and asked him "Who told you, you could be out here working?"

I don't remember what name he used, must not had been someone important because Spanky told him I don't want to ever see you out here again. If I come back and your still here, you will be talking to my rottweilers. I laughed my ass off when duded looked at Spanky then down at his dogs then back up at Spanky.

My block was definitely a mix of danger and humor.

CHAPTER 11

JOY RIDE

B usiness opportunities came a dime a dozen in those days; however, every opportunity wasn't a smart one. You had your hustlers who made money and invested back into their community and its people. Then there were the ones who only invested in themselves. The street was not loyal to anyone. I'm grateful that I was smart enough to see through all that even at that age.

Everyone on the block was making money one way or another, unlike me who started to have resentments. Not towards anyone who was on the rise to financial freedom but towards Beverly and Sam Jr. Just because Sam Jr. was around, he wasn't much of a father to me, guess his on again off again mentally had to do.

Never was there anything consistent about our relationship. Not because I didn't want it to be, lord knows I wanted and needed it to me.

It takes a real man to dig deep inside their heart to find the compassion needed to raise a child. Sam Jr was not that man.

Beverly well she was still incarcerated and how can a woman really be a mother from the behind the walls, not that she wanted to be anyway. Makes you wonder why many young men who come out of Harlem turned to the street. I made my friends on the block my friend and since most of my male cousins were in the block too it was easy for me to plunge right into the lifestyle. Ty was one of my closet cousins he always had my back and I mean always had my back. I could do no wrong in his eyes. No matter what I did his spankings were always filled with a jewel.

The customers who came into town to cop those 200 quarters at a time to take back to their hometowns were now copping to get high themselves. They would pull up get there fix and then go into one of the many shooting galleries in the hood. I recognize one of Ty customer he drove up parked his car and walked around looking for Ty when he found him, they had a short conversation and the next thing I know Ty had the keys to his ride.

I was super hype because I knew I was going to get those keys eventually. Ty drove around the hood for a about a day or so he then questioned his custy about the money he owed him he tried to tell him he needed to go to the bank and kept running his tag up. Ty was not falling for the bullshit so he then handed the keys over to me and told me to sell it so he could re-coup his money.

The owner of the car was so involved with getting high that he wasn't worried about his car.

I was already a seasoned driver because back in my survival days D. Boss, Timbo and I use to steal the mail trucks from the post office on Gerard Avenue.

I took one look at the shiny black thunderbird with red leather seats and sunroof and jumped right in. I was gone for 3 days joy riding all over Harlem, up and down the avenues, block by block I made my presence known yet ducking Ty at the same time. I slept in the car at night when the sun went down and then did it all over again in the morning. Hiding the car, I would head to Aunt Mary's house to freshen up then I would hit the road again.

I was ballin' at least I thought I was till Ty started looking for me. I got the word that Ty was on the hunt. Guess when the owner was not able to pay his tab, he left the block and reported the car stolen.

Riding down Lenox Ave on the uptown side with the song; "Ain't no stopping us now" by McFadden and Whitehead on blast I saw a crowd of people in front of Harlem World on 116th street. I made a quick U-turn on 117th St. and headed back in that direction. I call myself stuntin' and parked by the 2 train when two transit police officers came up the stairs and noticed me. One of them made a hand gesture for me to lower the music. I complied then became hesitant when they asked me for my license and registration. I reached over to the glove compartment handed them over the registration but when asked who owned the car, I couldn't tell them that because I didn't know.

Unfortunately, I was arrested that night for Grand Larceny I felt so stupid because how the fuck did, I let transit bust me. All I had to do was pull off. What were they going to do chase me?

The officers took me to a Precinct at the subway station on 145th St. Upon arrival I felt a little leery I thought I knew all of the local police stations little did I know that there was a police station there.

This was my first encounter with the law as an adult the process was different, there were no more phone calls to mommies telling her to come pick up their child. There were no more family courts stepping in to save the day. This time around I was going through the system. Something I was not ready for yet was ready if that makes sense.

I was put in a room where a detective came in after a few minutes with a pen and paper and was asked to make a statement. Since day one of meeting Cliff and hanging out around Ty, I was told on more than one occasion that if I was stopped by the police, I was never to talk to them. I was never to tell on the block, I was not to tell on myself. All those teachings of the basic street codes came into play as I sat there with a sarcastic grin on my face.

I thought it was funny when the detective became frustrated when he realized he was not getting any information from me.

I just stared pass him, sat on a cold ass steel chair and fold my arms across my chest. He thought he was scaring me by telling me that I was going up top for a long time if I didn't tell him where I got the car from. He told me that the car was reported stolen by a Mrs. something or other and that in order to save myself I had to tell him the truth. I never said a word, in my mind I was getting out of there until I didn't.

I was processed by the booking officer who asked me my name age and address. I didn't feel like I had to deny them that information, at the end of the day, I just wanted to hurry up and get out of there. I was really angry at the system because after they built my pedigree with the information, I gave them. I was headed to Central Booking, the Tombs Criminal Court no matter what you called it; it was all the same shit 100 Centre Street.

CHAPTER 12

THE TOMBS

The tombs originally known as the hall of justice is located at 125 White street in the Chinatown section of Manhattan, it's an extension of the criminal courthouse where they hold felony and misdemeanor offenders who are awaiting on an arraignment; the formal act of going in front of a judge to have one's case decided.

The ride down to the courthouse seemed like a one-way ticket to hell, it was hot, I hadn't slept and the officers wouldn't shut the fuck up. I was ready to get this over with and head back to the block. I knew that Ty must have been heated and I had to go show face. He might not had known that I got locked up but then again, he should have. There were so many people out there on 116th when I was arrested.

It took the arresting officers a minute to take me to the precinct, they had called in for a backup squad to come and snatch me up while they collected the evidence, the vehicle.

So, I knew Ty must had gotten the word already.

When we took exit 2, Manhattan civic center off of the FDR drive I began to sweat profusely, I didn't know what to expect and when you're in the dark about something that can take your stress to the next level. I asked the officers if they knew how long I was going to be at the courthouse they gave me very little information. I had to ride this out blindly and hope that it would only be a few hours before I was out of there.

Once at the courthouse I was handed over to another officer who wore that same blue uniform, but the patches were different. I was immediately escorted into a dingy hallway and up a set a stair that lead to some holding cells where there were other detainees spread out on the floor sleeping. I noticed a dude on the phone talking loud as though to be noticed, the conversation was obviously with a woman, his tone was super aggressive and his words harsh, I thought to myself as the first officer handed the second officer a folder, if a nigga had to go through all that to get his woman to do the right thing by him, he was going about it the wrong way.

The holding cell officer told me to walk over to a wooden stand where he fingerprinted me, spread each finger onto black ink then onto a card with my name on the top. He then pointed to a wall with a poster taped to it, there is where he took a photo of me looking towards the camera then a side view photo. At that point I started to realize that I was playing with the big boys. Being that it was the first time I went through anything like this, everything I had anticipated was not going to be. These police officers were building a profile on me a record of the arrest, they were making a record for future identification purposes.

Once that process was completed, I was handed a brown paper bag with a sandwich and a small carton of milk. I knew once I unwrapped that sandwich that I was not going to eat it.

I got lucky though when I looked at the bottom of the bag and found an apple, come to find out that the trustees would take the apples out of the bags and take them back to their units.

There wasn't a clock in sight I didn't know how long I had been sitting on the wooden bench all I knew was the bones on my backside was starting to hurt. No matter how I positioned my small frame I was uncomfortable. My stress level was over the top, half of the men that were in that particular cell were kicking heroin.

Withdrawal symptoms was common in the hood I would hear the heroin addicts complain about how their bones ached and they needed a fix to relieve that pain before it got worst however, they were out on the street and they were able to get their next hit. In that cell I had witnessed men who were reduced to nothing. The officers didn't care that they were moaning complaining, they did give a fuck that they had nausea abdominal pain, sweats, muscle spasms and the worst one of all, diarrhea. They didn't care that they had me in the mix of all of that. The stench coming from the toilet bowl which sat in the corner open for everyone to see was becoming unbearable it was hot as hell and the window which measured about 2 x 2 inches across the top of the wall close to the ceiling didn't help. I paced back and forth trying to get away from the smell. I went up to the gate and called out to the officer I yelled out that I needed to be moved out of that cell and into another one.

I waited a few seconds but no one answered me, I began to yell louder then finally an officer walked over and told me to get away from the gate or he would make my file disappear and I wouldn't see the judge any time soon.

How fucked up is that? I cursed his ass out continued to yell out for nothing. I wasn't moved anywhere I was stuck in there.

I went to sit back down before I could stop myself, I had dozed off. I overheard a conversation with the officer and some inmates who had come to serve the detainee's breakfast. Officers told them to cover their noses because the cells were offensive and needed to be cleaned out. Suddenly they walked over to the cell and told us to get our asses up. We were escorted into another cell while they attempted to clean the one, we were in.

Time was going slow I was anxious I could hear my heart beat through my chest. Tears formed on the corners of my eyes as I thought about Aunt Mary. If for one second, I could just get her to get me the hell out of there. Although I was a teenager now, I still felt the need to have her in my corner I looked over at the pay phone, I needed to call her call, or anyone that had any type of interest in me, but I didn't have 10 cents nor did I remember anyone numbers.

I felt alone and abandoned once again there was no one, no one but me and my demons.

There was no difference between the new cell and the old one. I started to become disruptive a thing I use to do whenever I didn't want to feel. I had a lighter on me because back then we were able to smoke cigarettes. I took the lighter climbed up the iron bars and burnt my name onto the ceiling.

Then I turned around and carved a scripture into the wall
(Sammy O was here and now he is gone he left this scripture
to carry on. Those who read it read well, those who don't go
the hell.)

I wrote that for the brothers who come after me to let them
know that they were not the only ones who take this journey.

Maybe two or three hours after that my name was called,
I thought it was over but there was a few more steps into the
process.

A medium size white gentleman walked up to the gate in
a wrinkled suit, a white-collar shirt with a bow tie he also had
on glasses that hung on the tip of his nose. In his left hand
he held a briefcase and, in his right, he held my folder. He
told me that I would be going in front of the judge soon and
that the judge was going to ask a few questions, first one being
what would be my plead, he told me that he was going to say
that I was not guilty and move on from there.

Upon entering the court room, the palms of my hand
became moist I was nerves yet tried my best to show no fear. I
walked over to a wooden table and stood behind it as the clerk
stated my charges to the judge. My lawyer leaned into me
and told me that today was my lucky day. Judge Bruce wright
AKA Cut Loose Bruce was presiding and it was rumored that
he was a fair man when it came to the African American and
Hispanic communities. He looked down at the paperwork
than took one look at me then told the district attorney that
he was going to release me on my own recognizance. Which
meant that I didn't have to pay bail all I had to do was sign a
written promise to appear in court as required.

I was confused didn't have a clue as to what they were
talking about. My attorney noticed the look on my face and

told me you will be going home today but you have to come back on the date they put on the calendar. Those words were like music to my ears I would have promised just about anything to get the hell out.

I signed on the dotted line and walked right out that court room.

CHAPTER 13

CUT LOOSE BRUCE

Once I left the court room, I practically ran down the hall towards the exit, my heart was racing, I wanted nothing more than to get out of there before the judge changed his mind.

I could hear my attorney calling out my name from behind me as he rushes towards me. I remember trying to get out the revolving doors before he could reach me. I didn't know what he wanted and I wasn't trying to find out after what I had went through the night before. I needed to get out of there and back to my comfort zone.

At this point I had stopped worrying about what Ty was going to say about my three-day joy ride. To be completely honest I welcomed his wrath.

The attorney stood in front of me and handed me some forms guess it was my copies of the agreement to report back to court. I remember him telling me the date and time of my next court appearance however I paid him no attention. I didn't have any intentions of coming back to court. I had already decided that the minute the judge let me go. If they wanted me, they would have to find me. I took the documents out of his hand, told him ok, but not before I asked the attorney for a dime so I could make a phone call.

I practically ran out of the courthouse when I exited the building, I took a deep breath filled my lungs with fresh air and headed to a phone booth.

I need to say that I was really immature at sixteen and my thought process was definitely off. I thought I was doing something slick, something impressive when my first phone call was to the Touch of Class Car service.

I waited for my car for about twenty minutes when it arrived, I jumped in leaned back and smiled, a smile of relief.

That ride back uptown was smooth I stared out the window as I tried to put my explanation to Ty into words. He was going to get on me and he had every right. I already knew that no matter what I told him he was not going to be alright with what I did.

I pulled up to block the vision of the guys out there still doing what they do made me realize that the show must go on with or without me. Times were changing and I was alright with that, I couldn't dwell on the fact that my boys were not going to baby me anymore once I caught that case, I became man in their eyes.

Everything I went through in my life made me stronger. I saw Ty standing in front of my building I got out of the car and walked right up to him. I handed him the court papers and started to give him an explanation.

He cut me off and told me "I saw your ass nigga I tried to call out to you, but you had the music so damn loud you didn't hear me. I also saw when the police rolled up on you there was nothing I could do. I don't understand why the hell you would take it upon yourself to put yourself in a compromising position. You must have gasoline on your chest."

I just looked at him, there was no point in trying to debate with him. I bowed down only because I had respect for him. He handed me the paperwork back and stated

"You better go back to court we don't need the police out here looking for you."

I chilled for a few weeks went back to court and received three years' probation. Several things happen in that case that I was not aware of, first thing was that the transit police officers never read me my Miranda rights and the second thing was that I was still considered a minor.

I legally still lived with my guardian aunt Mary and by law the courts could not assign legal responsibility to an individual who lacks the metal capacity or maturity to fully understand the consequences of their action. When I took that car and rode around the neighborhood, I wasn't mature enough to think about any consequences. I was having fun, I felt important, grown, I was showing off.

If someone would have gone to court with me, I'm sure that the outcome would have been different then again maybe not.

It's like the saying goes everything happens for a reason.

I never reported to probation like I was suppose too but what I did do was continue to run the streets and play the hand that I dealt. Although my mind was still in the development stages my body was ahead of it time for sure.

Thomasina Bell was proof of that when I noticed her walk pass Loray's I thought she was the most beautiful girl I had ever seen. I made a comment out loud about her beauty and to my surprise she stopped and looked at me. That was my chance to talk to her. I asked her where she was from and she told me that she was from the Bronx it was a coincidence that she was also from Gerard Ave.

We hit it off right away and because I wanted to get off my block, I started going to the Bronx more often to see her, and of course to see my family. D. Boss and Timbo always looked for ways to get into something. But I only wanted to get into Thomasina. This was a whole new experience for me. Sure, I had gotten a taste of a woman when Ty forced me into that room with that hoe but that was just sex, what I had with Thomasina was different. It was intimacy we talked about everything she wanted to know all about me and that was a first. She made me feel comfortable so much so that I was able to share with her my situation with my aunt Mary without feeling embarrassed about it. I broke it down to the core, I told her about all the problems I was having with my living situation.

Don't get me wrong Aunt Mary couldn't help herself when she was sober, she was the sweetest woman in the world but when she got that liquor in her she turned into someone else and took it out on me. Basically, one minute she wanted me in the house and the next she would throw me out. As time went on her addiction got worst so did the nights I spent out on the street. I never had a stable moment in my life until Thomasina. One night as I walked her home, she asked me where I was going to spend the night. The season was changing quickly so it was started to get chilly outside.

I didn't even know how to answer that I always managed to rest my head somewhere. I just didn't know where I was going that night.

Thomasina told me to wait up she went into her building then came back out with her sister Ann and brother Black Leroy. They came up with a plan to sneak me into their house. Thomasina had a long walk-in closet in her room and there is where I slept. One night turned into two then three and so on.

Everyone at her house knew I was staying there except her mother. Late in the evening I would sneak in, sleep in the closet and when her mother would go to work, I would jump into Thomasina's bed.

There wasn't one day that went by that I didn't fuck her. She was so into me that she found ways for us to be together. She was at my disposal for the taking, neither one of us were virgins but we were each other's first in many ways. My feelings grew for her with each day that passed I was falling in love for the first time. Making love with her was like attending a private school I learn to touch, kiss, and keep her interested in me and what I had to give her. She reciprocates my every move; our relationship was filled with passion with a twist of mental stimulation. I would love to get raw with it but to keep it clean and respectful the bottom line is that we thugged it out in the bedroom.

How I knew I had fallen hard for her was when I   was separated from her by getting myself caught up in some bullshit.

I had gone to Harlem one day to hang out and to check up on Aunt Mary. When I was on my way back to the Bronx, I ran into Wayne, Johnny toughs' older brother. He was the neighborhood bully and I was scared of him he came out of

143rd St on 7th Avenue. He had a reputation for patting niggas down and taking their belongings. When he called me out, I started running I ran across the bridge on 145th and into the Bronx as though my life depended on it. Crazy thing is that Wayne ran after me he didn't let up either. I don't know what he thought I had because I didn't have nothing of value. I continued to run towards my cousins' house when I got there, I noticed that Wayne was still on my tail. I ran up the stairs where my cousins Val and Kat were sitting in the living room. I ran through the door out of breath and collapse from exhaustion.

My female cousins were no joke remember what I said in the beginning of my story, the women in my family had a voice and their voice cut deep when need be. They jumped at attention and asked what happen when I tried to tell them all they heard was me stating that Wayne had chase me to the Bronx all the way from Harlem.

We all went downstairs to see if he was still around. Kat insisted that I fight him, she told me that in order to get over your fear you had to face it head on.

Wayne was halfway up the block when we yelled out to him, bold ass nigga turned around and headed back towards me. Once he got close enough, I whaled on his ass it turns out that he wasn't that tough after all. I whipped his ass and to celebrate that evening in the middle of the street I let off two shots in the air from my Cousin Val's gun and I got arrested.

CHAPTER 14

RIKER'S ISLAND

Here I go again! Having to go through the whole process of being booked, arraigned and sentenced for celebrating my victory was a slap in the face. The things we did in the hood to prove ourselves was beyond ignorant but we did it anyway. This time around the process was longer due to me never showing up to probation. This time around the attorney assigned to my case wasn't very enthusiastic about working with me. You can see it in his face and the tone in his voice was that of an individual who didn't believe I deserved a chance, so I was doomed before the court case had even began.

I was charged with possession of a weapon, unlawful discharge of a firearm and violation of probation.

My attorney had advised me to not wait for the inevitable. No matter how I wanted to avoid it I wasn't going home this time, I was crushed.

At arraignment, the district attorney's office offered me two to six years in a State correctional Facility. Those numbers knocked me off my feet, not because I couldn't do the time, it was because of Thomasina she was all I thought about as I sat in the bull pens awaiting transportation to Rikers Island.

Once the Bus arrived, I was shackled then escorted throughout central booking as the officers picked up all the others who were on their transport list

All of the stories I had heard from some of my boys who have been at Riker's Island were disturbing. There were no rules on the island the inmates ran the units and officers allowed it. They didn't care about what went down in the facility as long as their count was right, and no one got assaulted an hour before they punched out.

I held my composure as the bus made its way through the Bronx and across the Tri-Borough Bridge. My mind kept drifting in and out of reality although I was headed into the belly of the beast, I had to stand on my own I no longer had the support of the block. I had to grow up and grow up fast I had to push all of my insecurities to the side. I didn't know what to expect but whatever came my way I had to handle my business.

The bus started making its way across the Riker's Island Bridge, I was very observant of my surrounding now more than ever. I noticed that there was one lane going into the island and only one lane to come out. It was gloomy dark and raining I stared at the East river that ran between the Bronx and Queens. I heard airplanes passing by above me I was entering a whole new world.

When we finally made our way through the island, I seen several facilities some for the basic criminals and some for the criminally insane. We had finally reached C74 they called out my name I said a silent prayer, got up and walked to the front of the bus. There were about fifteen other detainees who were also going into that building, once we were all out of the bus we were hurdled in like cattle and place in the, WHY ME PEN.

We had to go through intake, medical and housing that took several hours but it felt like days. When we were all cleared to be housed, we were sent with an officer that was working as the escort officer for evening.

We came upon a long corridor with several openings divided by steel doors behind those steel doors was what they called the block or the building.

The corridor walls were grey and the arrows which directed the way to different sections of the jail were colored in green. I walked quietly down the hallway holding a blanket rolled up with a white sheet, cup, and a toothbrush and if you got lucky a small tube of toothpaste, I happened to get lucky. I can feel the pressure coming on, here is where I had to prove myself, here is where I had to make a name for myself everything that I had learned on 111th St. was now going to be put to the test.

"Yo! Sammy you go in here." I took one look at the receiving officer who took my card and said to myself "Here we go let the games begin."

It was late at night, so the building was dimly lit but that didn't stop me from absorbing every inch of the structured cement and steel box. There were plastic tables and chairs in the center of the floor with cell doors against the walls I saw the phones on one side of the room behind a gate and the shower stalls on the other. Officer told me to go in front of cell number twenty-five so he could open the door. Upon entering the cell, I found a mattress that laid on top of a steel frame a toilet bowl and a stainless-steel sink and let's not forget the fun house mirror that was screwed into the wall. There was a small window that overlooked a deserted courtyard. My first impression was that of a bathroom with a bed in it.

My first full day on Rikers began by me missing breakfast, it was around 4 am when the officers started to open the cell doors so the inmates could make their way to the mess hall. The officers were adamant about us being by the door when they made their rounds if you weren't, they would continue on to the next. I was too tired to get up anyway but by lunch time I was up and ready to go. I could feel my stomach cramping that feeling wasn't new to me I knew hunger pains all to well. As I stood by the door waiting to be let out, I heard the other guys talking through the vents. To be honest listening to them was how I got most of the information I needed to get through the day.

"On the chow on the chow!" Doors opened and shut quickly I looked through the glass on my door, watched as all of the inmates lined up. When it was my turn I walked out of the cell as though I had done this a million times before.

It was never about how many times a person got locked up, it was about how they handled themselves when they did.

CHAPTER 15

C74

All eyes were on me as I entered the mess hall at least I thought they were. Every afternoon the inmates who weren't housed at C74 5 upper, scanned the chow line to see who had come into the facility. Newbies were processed into the jail at all hours of the day and night, intake was never closed down, the city made sure of that.

No one recognized me, no one shouted out my name talking about I GOT YOU like I heard the other do that was because I wasn't Sammy O yet. I was just another face in the crowd, and I had to admit that I was scared to death.

I stood on that line with my heart in my throat. I kept my head held high; my eyes focused on the things that was happening around me. I too scanned the room for a friendly face, no one. I couldn't show signs of weakness that was not acceptable in that environment. I kept it cool, I tried to remain focused I tried to gather my strength as I continued to watch the others. I thought about the block Ty, Cliff and all of the jewels they had shared with me.

Then suddenly my demeanor gradually began to change. I could hear Ty's voice play out in my head as he told me on so many occasions.

"No matter how scared you may be, never allow anyone to see your fear. They will use that shit against you."

I started to get comfortable in that space. I had to let go of my insecurities take everything I learned on the streets and bring it into this situation. The rules never changed no matter where you are in life. With each situation I had to learn to adapt without compromising my manhood or my reputation.

As the line moved forward, I followed suit its chicken day and the inmates were wilding out. Their voices echo throughout the room loudly. The officers posted up on each side of the mess hall were at attention.

The mess hall was set up with rows of tables in the center of the space separating one housing unit from the other but that didn't stop them from screaming out to each other.

Then suddenly heard my name being yelled out from across the room. I turned in the direction of the voice, I saw my cousin waving his hand at me.

Finally, a friendly face my cousin Jimmy, D. Boss's older brother the one that had been in and out of jail for as long as I could remember. Although we weren't that close, we were family.

"Yo! Sammy O you alright?" Jimmy yelled out.

I wasn't sure if I could yell back but I did, letting him know that I was okay. My cousin was short and stocky but big in life, from the looks of things he had a lot of pull in the jail system, and the way that he spoke with so much authority let me know that he was running his block and that everyone respected him. He barked orders from across the room he informed some of the men in my block to look out for me to make sure that no one fucked with me.

Believe it or not that made me feel at ease. To know that I had someone looking out for me where there was no one looking out for me.

I only stayed on the Rikers Island for about two weeks then I was packed up and sent to Elmira correctional Facility the only facility in the county for adolescences, which was about four hours away from New York City. On that ride up north I had a chance to do a lot of thinking. I thought about Aunt Mary, Thomasina, Beverly and of course I thought about Sam Jr. I thought about all the times I needed my family and they were not there for me. I thought about how I ended up on the street looking for things I should've found at home. Those thoughts made me get emotional, however, I didn't let it get the best of me, I had to brush those thoughts out of my head toughen up. I had to get through this.

"Welcome to Elmira! Failure to follow our rules and regulations, we will be forced to take you down. You are no longer a name so remember your number because that is how you will be identified." The state correction officer barked into my face.

He continued on to say "This is not Rikers Island I don't care what you did down there we have our own rules here. There will be a rule book upon admission make sure you memorize it and don't' lose it because you will have to pay for it!"

We were taken inside where we were ordered to strip, I was humiliated I never stripped in front of other people like that before. It was the first time in my life that I was exposed completely, vulnerable to the system. The abuse, which is my interpretation continued, they sprayed us down with a chemical that they claimed killed lice. Only God knows what that spray was all about. And be mindful we were not allowed to ask questions or speak to the officers unless we were being spoken to.

I overheard some of the men whispering to each other about the time they had gotten for their crimes, anywhere from ten to twenty-five years to life those individuals I thought after hearing them brag were already mentality ready for their consequences.

Unlike me, I was blessed that no one was hurt during my standoff with Wayne or when I shot that gun in the air. That little two to six years was considered a skid bid to a brother who was sentenced to a lot of time. I was cursed and blessed at the same time, what I did with my time is what mattered, not what the time would do to me.

Subconsciously my spirit was broken but I couldn't let anyone know this.

The intake process was definitely different from the city jails to the state prisons. I took a mandatory shower after being sprayed down like an animal I was given four uniforms (greens) with my name and din numbers visibly across the left side of the shirt, they gave me t-shirts, underwear, socks, coat and pair of black boots. I was then taken to the barber shop where they shaved my head and facial hair. I was housed at B Block reception for a day then transferred to A Block, once again I had to adapt to being locked down for about thirty days only going to the mess hall, medical, education assessment and the yard.

Upon entering the housing unit, I could hear an inmate screaming from his cell "New Jack, Yo! We got a new jack!" suddenly the whole unit chimed in, into a combined harmonious rant, Yeah, I was the new jack but I wasn't going to act like one. I had already put it in my mind that I was going to follow protocol while creating some of my own.

We were only allowed one phone call a month but the visiting floor was open to everyone, I was not stressing the phone calls to much because the one phone call I had I made it to Aunt Mary. I asked her to get me a few things like a food package and some clothes. Wasn't sure if she could do it but I asked anyway in hopes that she could.

Several days later they called out my name I was so excited when they told me that I had a visit. I couldn't wait to see Aunt Mary I knew that it took a lot for her to travel all those hours to see me, especially in her condition. When I arrived at the visiting floor, I was surprised to see Thomasina sitting at the table alongside my aunt. My heart dropped I really didn't expect her to come see me. To see the two women that I loved more than anything in the world meant so much to me.

Although we were strictly confined to a table, we found ways to make my visit entertaining by playing board games, cards, taking photos and eating.

You know I was super happy when my greedy ass found out that I could get food out of the vending machine. I ate burgers, chips and drank sodas at the beginning of the visit, then went back for more during the visit. Our conversation was light we talked about the block the people that lived in and all the general shit that we thought was important, but really wasn't. I had a lot of questions and concerns about what would happen to me and who would be there for me throughout this bid. I didn't want to do to it alone. I needed my family for sure. This is why when Thomasina told me that she was going to do this bid with me it was like music to my ears. It's crazy because I didn't ask her to do so, all of her promises to wait for me came out of her which makes it all the more meaningful.

You see when incarcerated we tend to put expectations on people to only be disappointed. I was already disappointed in myself I was already kicking myself in the ass for being so reckless. I didn't need the added stress from the outside world.

Thomasina expressed to me that she loved me and that she couldn't see herself without me. I was relieved to hear those words I loved her too. She was my first love the first woman that made me feel special. She had proven herself when she took me into her house, hind me from her mother, defied her mother's rules just to make sure I had a place to rest my head.

So, I believed her.

Aunt Mary assured me that she would be there for me too. I left that visit feeling secure yet touched by a little sadness.

I held the tears that were beginning to form in the corners of my eye as I walked back to my unit. But once I walked into my cell and heard the door slam behind me, I cried.

CHAPTER 16

ELMIRA

I was packed and moved to Coxsackie a few days after my visit, shackled yet again and being thrown onto a bus started to take its toll on me. I hoped that this would be the last time that I would be transferred because I needed to settle in and start doing my time.

Different prison same rules that's what I assumed due to the rule book I read from beginning to end, then read again. There wasn't much to do during the reception period at Elmira so why not familiarize myself with what was expected of me.

Now six hours away from home I had to go through the same routine when I had arrived at Elmira, that process was becoming redundant.

I didn't have a clue that I was being sent to a prison that was designed for adolescents.

My attorney left that out at sentencing.

New York State department of corrections classified me as a high-risk offender at the age of 16 years old, although

I was too young to be in an adult facility, I was still what people called prison material, so I had to be put somewhere, so coxsackie it was.

I would rather be around guys my own age any way, not that they didn't have their fair share of horror stories. I was still willing to take my chances.

Coxsackie was a tough prison the officers were very strict we weren't allowed to do anything guess that was their way of telling us to never come to prison. But their tactics were that of mental abuse. Never physical unless one of the inmates got out of hand but abuse still the same.

They wanted to be in control of our every being and I started to realize that there was something wrong with that. The prison was ran like a lockdown facility. I spent so many hours in my cell that I thought I would lose my mind at times. There was but so much I could do in there and of course the other inmates felt the same way. How could we not feel alone, depressed and under distress we were only teenagers, and no one knew what went on in our lives to get us there. The worse part was that the system didn't care to know. All they knew was that we were found guilty of a crime and they were the ones who was going to punish us not rehabilitate us which is what the majority of us needed.

On my way to chow one day I noticed a white officer who had the markings of a lynched black baby on his upper bicep. I stared at that tattoo as though the offense was made directly towards to me. I thought about Homer and his experience with racism although at the time I didn't take him seriously, I started to now. Now that I saw it with my own eyes now that I felt it within my soul.

How I was being treated was unacceptable and I was going to do something about it. I began to make a list of all the things I felt needed to be changed not because I wanted to run the prison but because I felt like I was living in modern day slavery. Every chance I got be it in the yard, showers and through kites I started to tell the others that in order for things to change for us we had to do something major, disturbing, something that would make the system respect us as human beings. We had to assemble, come together as a team.

As they did in the Attica riot, I came across an article in a magazine where they described that on September 9, 1971 nearly thirteen hundred prisoners took over Attica Correctional Facility in Upstate New York to protest years of mistreatment. Holding guards and civilian employee hostage, the prisoners negotiated with officials for improved conditions during the four long days and nights that followed. The article was about a woman by the name of Heather Ann Thompson who was working on a book by the name of Blood in The Water. Official decided not to listen to the prisoners and instead take back their prison causing inmates and civilians to be killed during their take over.

I didn't want to go that route, so I came up with putting together a food strike.

While I was coordinating the strike, I continued to get my visits with Aunt Mary on a regular. She had no idea just how much does visits kept me sane. Being on the visits with her gave me a sense of normalcy.

It was June 13th 1981 when Aunt Mary surprised me with Thomasina, it was my birthday weekend so I was happy to see her. On this visit, I expressed to Aunt Mary my concern about how I was being treated. I didn't tell her that I was planning a food strike because I didn't want her to worry but I did give her a list of things that I wasn't comfortable with. Thomasina and I talked as well, but our conversation was based on our relationship. She had expressed to me how she wished she could come more often to see me, how she missed me, how she loved me etc.

On that day three days before my birthday was the last time, I seen Thomasina during my incarceration. I always thought of her sent letters and sent messages with Aunt Mary, but I never heard from her again. After about a year into my bid I received a letter from my cousin D. Boss who was also locked up he had been sent to a juvenile center somewhere upstate.

In that letter he wrote that Thomasina was pregnant that she had been seeing someone else and that she had no intentions on seeing me again. I was broken hearted as the letter slipped from my hands and onto the floor. Imagine getting a letter like that while your lockdown in a cell for twenty-three hours of the day. There was nowhere to go nor anyone to talk to, I had to eat that shit. The most devasting part of the whole letter was when D-Boss told me that she was pregnant from his brother my cousin, my family Mark. I felt that pain in the pit of my stomach. Anyone who has ever had a broken heart before knows what I was talking about.

That Dear John letter created so much pain and anger in me that all I wanted to do was lash out, and the only outlet I had at the time was the wall that stood in front of me. I punched that wall so fucking hard I broke my hand.

From that day forward I turned into someone else I could feel the transformation and I embraced it. I started to change emotionally at first and then physically. I was becoming someone that I sometimes didn't even recognize myself. I was done with being that sweet little boy everyone on the streets portrayed me to be. My thoughts my voice then my body followed in the transformation. I spent so much time alone that it was easy for me to get into my own head. I promised myself that I was only going to do two days in prison the day I walked in and the day I walked out.

Once my hand healed, I started to work out twenty push up turned into one hundred sits up and dips quickly shifted my body in a new direction. My mental was no longer being controlled by the officer either this was my time to do and I was going to do it my way. I wasn't scared of nothing anymore whatever came my way came. I was physically and mentally ready to pursue my rights.

The unit porters were the main source of my strength without them I would not have been able to round up and organize the date for the food strike. The whole unit had to be down with it or it would have been pointless, anyone who wasn't willing to participate would be burnt out which means their cells would be set on fire.

On the day of the food strike we formed a line and headed to the mess hall in union. We picked up our trays walked pass the mess hall workers and sat down at the tables with empty trays and only our forks in our hand. When I realized that I could actually have 30 individuals follow me on command I realized that I was becoming a leader.

A leader is one who knows the way, goes the way and shows the way.

To recognize that I had that type of power was to recognize that on that day Samuel died and Sammy O was born!

CHAPTER 17

SHIPPED OUT

E very action has a reaction thinking back at the situation now I learn that when you poke the bear the bear will poke you back.

They packed my ass up so fast I didn't know what hit me. That food strike didn't accomplish anything with the administration, the only thing I got out of that experience was a one-way ticket back to Elmira. Although, I was able to organize a food strike with my fellow convicts that shit didn't last long. Some of them bailed out on the cause only leaving nine other inmates and myself. That was alright though because I was desperate to get out of Coxsackie. That ride back felt like I was going home. Elmira was a gladiator school for inmates, there was always something going on and to me that was exciting. There wasn't one day that the men weren't forced to become prisoners of war.

I was already in that space mentally; I was physically getting stronger with each passing day. My voice compelled attentiveness, trust, and respect, true leadership qualities. I presented a strong presence whenever I walked into a room.

It didn't take long for me to have a reputation in Elmira even though it wasn't a positive rep my name held weight making it easy for others to follow me. I build a small crew of only niggas from Harlem and the Bronx there was about eight of us at first and as they came into the facility our crew became bigger. Our motto was that we took care of our own no matter what there was no judgement. Only thing that wouldn't get you a pass was if you were labeled a snitch with tangible proof that you were one.

I made it my business to know who was who, in the facility. If you worked in the mess hall, I wanted to touch base with who ran it. If you worked in the state shop, I wanted to know who ran that and so on and so on.

I wanted to be in direct contact with the boss the one who could make all the decisions.

It was only a matter of time that I would get myself caught up in a lot of bullshit, how could I not, I was being raised by the system. I didn't care about getting tickets or being in key lock, I had something to prove, my reputation preceded me.

So basically, you didn't have to meet me to know what I was about. I was becoming a stand-up loyal nigga whose word was bond. I had come along way.

I wasn't that scrawny nappy headed kid who sat on the sidelines waiting for a break I became the one who gave the breaks. Everyone in my crew was straight they ate good they slept well but most of all I put them all in positions where they could help out the next brother coming in from our hood.

I worked various of jobs that allowed me to move around the facility easily, working in the clinic as a porter, working with the civilians gave an advantage most inmates didn't have.

Two years into my bid and all of the work I had put into establishing myself at Elmira came to an end. Early one morning I was called down to the administration building by my counselor. I thought the worst because it was rare when a counselor called you down to their office. I thought about Aunt Mary as I made my way to admin. I prayed that she was okay because I wasn't ready to hear any bad news.

"Mr. Samuel, I called you down here to let you know that your request for a transfer has been approved."

I would be packed up yet again and transferred out.

I thought I was going to Fishkill, Mid Orange or Woodburn which were all closer to the city. I did put in a request for a transfer I few weeks prior in hopes of getting closer to home, the closer I got to the city the more visits I would get, and you already know how important those visits are.

Honestly, I didn't know if they would even consider it with my prison record. Technically when an inmate received tickets (infractions) they could lose privileges or worst they could lose their draft status so when my counselor told me I was being shipped out I was surprised.

I was already planning my transfer out of Elmira in my head. Since I had already made a name for myself throughout the prison system, I had to make sure my peoples had gotten word that I may end up in one of the three prisons I have mentioned. So, I sent word with some of the other guys that were being drafted out before me.

The bus traveled on several different roads making its way downstate. I couldn't wait to get there, wherever there, was. I still didn't know where I was being transferred to but wherever I ended up I knew that I would be alright. I looked forward to the move.

Five hours later the bus pulled up to a hospital, I was confused especially when some O.G.s started ranting about the place. They had never been there before nor had they ever heard about Pilgrim State, from the little information we were able to obtain Pilgrim State was a psychiatric Center that was converted into a state prison due to overcrowded conditions.

It was located in Brentwood N.Y. also known as Long Island although I was somewhat closer to home this was not where I wanted to be. I went from being able to roam Elmira my way, to being stuck in a building all day.

I could feel the crazy all around me. I was back to being secluded which made me stressed out. I had very little tolerance for bullshit. I was already feeling some type of way about being in a psychiatric center no matter what name they tacked onto the building, it was what it was.

My irritation was on over drive and I found myself lashing out on some of the officers.

The level of respect for the inmates was little to none. These officers were different they thought they could disrespect us by talking to us as though we were their sons. I had a maximum security mentally and respect meant everything.

If I didn't learn anything else in Elmira, I learned that everyone deserved some level of respect, until they didn't, but I demanded it.

There was a new officer on my unit, he was what we called a rookie. When in training they are taught to go strictly by the book and that's what he was doing.

He was making me feel uncomfortable. It was bad enough that I was locked down in a building with no movement whatsoever. This officer here was doing too much.

I was congregating with a bunch of dudes, just sitting around talking shit in a corner, when the rookie comes up to us and tells us that we had to break it up. I had a problem with authority especially when we did the same thing every day and no one else had a problem with it. We were minding our business doing what young men do. He repeated himself with a stern tone that's when I went off on him.

"Get the fuck out here man go find yourself something else to do!" apparently my tone shook him because the next thing I knew he had pulled the pin alerting orange crush a prison tack force who handled prison upraises. That was when Sgt. Hardy came into play. He arrived on the unit with about six other officers, the bomb squad in full affect. He asked the officer what happen officer told him his side of the incident. When it was my turn to explain He turned toward me then yelled into my face "Who the fuck are you to talk to my officers that way!"

Then he turned to another officer and asked for his cuffs. I was hand cuffed then walked out of the unit. Once we got in front of the freight elevator which would take me to the seventh floor (the box), I was stripped searched. They told me they were looking for a weapon, yeah okay, what they were really trying to do was humiliate me. They shoved me into the elevator completely naked. Then they twisted the light bulb off turned on a pocket flashlight, put a phone book over my head and hit me twice with a baton. Then suddenly the blows became rapid I could feel their punches, slaps, and kicks all over my body. I kept losing by breath as their boots connected with my ribs, I tried my best to curl up and hide myself from the ass whipping but they made sure they held me in a position where I could feel their wrath. I felt heat coming from the tip of toes to the top of my head I thought I was going to pass out then suddenly the doors slide open.

When the elevator door opened the officers now held me under each arm. They made sure that I wouldn't slide to the ground before they were able to tell the nurse that was now standing in front of us, their side of the story. From the look on her face I could see that she wouldn't believe them anyway because the only words that came out of her mouth before she reached out for me was "If you ever touch him again, I will not cover up for you."

I'm sure that this was not the first time she had seen an inmate brutally beaten at Pilgrim State, I'm also sure that it wasn't her last.

CHAPTER 18

SOLITARY CONFINEMENT

The Box

I t takes one minute to get in trouble, and it takes a lifetime to get out of it. That's what it felt like when I was handed down a sixty-day sentence in the box. Five day after the beat down by those officers I was escorted in front of the disciplinary community with a tier three ticket which is the worst ticket you can received in prison. It wasn't hard to see that I was hurt I walked in slowly due to my body being on fire. The bruises were more than visual too, yet they overlooked everything that was obvious and still gave me all that time.

I took that like a trooper, went back to my cell laid my ass down.

What else could I do? It didn't matter that I had my side of the story already rehearsed. When I tried to defend my institutional charge, they completely ignored me. It was all good though because I was in no shape to be on a regular unit anyway. There was no room for weakness. On a daily basis

I signed up for sick call (clinic) just to get out of my cell. I went there for varies things but mainly to get Tylenol which is the only pharmaceutical drug allowed. Anything stronger was out of the question. I started to heal, it had been about a month or so that I was confined to a small cell with only a bed toilet and sink. I started to get my body back into shape, my mental well they couldn't break me although they tried to do their best to do so. On one of those sick call runs the nurse on duty started to flirt with me she asked me to take off my shirt so she could take a look at my injuries, so she claimed. I laid back on the examining table and watched her has she touched poked and caresses my chest. She was more into my physique then preforming an appropriate exam. She pushed her titties into my face several time as she leaned into me. Woo wee if it would have been at another place and time, I probably would had gone for it, just because I was locked up didn't mean that my love for pussy had changed. She tried to entice me, but I saw that movie before, and I wasn't falling for that. I wasn't trying to get caught having sex with a civilian if you thought I got my ass whipped the first time imagine what they would have done to me this time.

I went back to my cell and as an afterthought I should had went for it. Early the next morning it was visiting day and I was waiting for Aunt Mary. I needed that visit to break up the monotony of being in solitary confinement for so long.

I was lucky enough to have my window facing the entrance of the institution. I paced the floor back and forth until I finally saw my aunt and another woman walk up to the gate. My heart was beating fast I was so happy to be getting out of that room. I watched them get buzzed in then make their way into a small building.

All I needed to do now was wait for an escort to take me down to the visiting floor. When I realized that they were taking too long I looked out the window again only to be disappointed to see Aunt Mary walking out of the prison. Suddenly I became enraged first thing that came to mind was that Sgt. Hardy had turned my visit away. There was no way for me to contact Aunt Mary because I had lost all of my privileges, so I had no choice but to lay down. Lucky for me three days later I was packed up and shipped the fuck out of there and back to Elmira.

When I got to Elmira the welcoming committee was front and center from the officers to my crew. Again, I was in my comfort zone. The officers threw out the remaining time I had in the box, so I got all of my privileges back and was housed in general population. The care packages from my boys came right on time just like I taught them. I was all set up and ready to finish off the rest of my bid, but there was something I had to do before things could move forward. I had to call my aunt Mary I wanted to know what happen the day that she was not able to get in to see me at Pilgrim state. Mainly I had to call her to let her know I was back at Elmira. I held a lot of animosity towards Sergeant Hardy because of what he did to me he was all I thought about. I was obsessed with wanting to see him again outside of those walls.

Aunt Mary had explained to me that she had been drinking that day, so she asked the woman she was with to come up to the visit with her. It turned out that the woman was Janice my cousin. She went on to tell me that they wouldn't let her into the facility because she was drunk, and Janice had a loose joint in her sock. I needed to get clarity; her explanation made me feel better about my family being turned away but it would never make me feel differently about Sergeant Hardy.

My journey through incarceration made my outlook on relationships very negative. Thomasina's betrayal hurt me to core it wasn't so much that she had moved on with her life it was who she moved on with. I trusted no one that's why I was leery when I met my homeboy Mumbles sister during an event most of the facility had by the name of Family Day. We all looked forward to that day because it was designed to provide inmates and their families the opportunity to enhance their family ties. At these events we were able to walk around, eat, take pictures, and play games. So much better than being confined to a table on the visiting floor. I smoked cigarettes at that time, on one of my smoke breaks I saw her.

"Yo! Mumbles who that?"

Mumbles quickly introduced her to me as his sister Janine. There were many females in the yard standing around with their peoples, but there was something about her that was different. She had a dope body and a personality to match. We talked briefly but my attention was on Aunt Mary who was standing right beside me. I kept it light until I was able to get Mumbles alone. I asked him about her again and to my surprise she wanted my name and numbers, so he hooked me up.

A few days later I received a letter from her, I wrote her back. We went from writing letters sending pics to phone calls. I began to open up to the idea of being with someone else and it felt good. She was very attentive towards me she wanted to know everything about me, and I wanted to know all about her too. My bid was running smoothly especially when I had something to look forward too. God was definitely on my side when once again I was packed up. This time I was not going to pack unless they told me where I was going, I refused. Since I had juice in the prison one of the inmates that worked in the receiving room looked out and told me I was going to Taconic Correctional, finally I would be forty-five minutes away from block.

Also, while at receiving I got the word that Ty was in the facility. I sent him a message to come to chow I was happy that I was going to have the chance to see him before I left. Elmira has two mess halls. Mess hall number one is population and mess hall number two was for reception. I was out of bound like a motherfucker, but I had to make sure my family was good. I entered the mess hall as though I belonged there. I scanned the area until he came into view, he was already sitting down eating I suddenly got off the line and walked directly towards him. Ty had an officer standing next to him when he saw me coming the officer began to back pedal away from Ty. I don't know what the officer thought I was going to do, but when I reached Ty, I hugged him. There was nothing like having a real homeboy in the building yeah, I had built friendships in the system but it couldn't compare to the one I had with Ty. I told him to play the yard that evening although I was packed up and ready to go in the morning, I had to make sure he was good.

Ty told me that evening that he saw the officer when he was backing up and found that odd. He too started to scan the mess hall to see if there was anyone coming their direction. Elmira was going through a race riot after JoJo's death, so you had to watch your back. But for an officer to back away instead of moving forward showed how dangerous Elmira really was. He also went on to tell me that he was glad it was me that ran up on him, because at the end of the end Ty was about his business too.

I handed Ty a care package, put him up on what was going on in the jail after that I made my way out of the yard but before I left I told him if you ever find that you have shit missing out your cell always step to the porter, they know everything that is going in the blocks.

Taconic was a medium facility, and they were not ready for me. I came down with that maximum-security attitude so when I saw that Taconic was the equivalent to club med, I was shell shock. They were so laid back I had to regroup and that didn't come easy to nigga like me. Many times, I had some O.G's Kojack, John Hayes and Scully all from Harlem pull me to side to tell me to calm down. My guards were always up, and I was always ready to fight. It was hard for me to relax but that's started to change when I started to get visits from Janine. She came to see me every weekend to make sure that I was good, Janine was holding me down.

I had two cousins that were at Taconic with me as well my cousin Pepsi (Pep) and my cousin Kid Kerry. I was really petty when it came to them if anyone dared to violate, I was always front and center to protect them I even would go as far as rigging basketballs games so they would win. I remember refereeing a game in the yard where my cousin Pepsi was playing. Whenever a player from the opposite team would touch him, I would call a foul. An onlooker was shouting derogatory remarks from a distance he was shouting out a little too much for my taste. I got so pissed I called referee official time out walked in his direction and commence to put the beats on him. When done I walked back blew the whistle and yelled out PLAY BALL. I found that shit funny yet not funny at all. I'm a Gemini so you never know what you're going to get when I feel disrespected. As time went on my time at Taconic became smooth, I started to relax. I was short now; I would be going home soon on my Conditional release date, so I focused my energy on planning my next move. But until then I tried to make my bid easier and that's when Ms. Robin came into play.

It was the last movement of the evening I had just finished working out at the gym, Ms. Robin must had been watching me because the minute I made my way out of the gym, up the stairs and into my room she was on me. I was dripping with sweat when she walked into my room reached out her hand to touch me. As a young man doing time in prison, a move like this was powerful. Powerful in many ways, although I didn't react to her touch, I did make it beneficial. That one move opened a pandoras box. There wasn't anything that she didn't do for me there were limits of course she wasn't going to jeopardize her job however anything that was feasible was done. She even went as far as telling the other female officers to look out for me too.

Laundry officer looked out Mess hall officer looked out Barbershop officer looked out. The only one that didn't and made my life impossible was the package room officer Ms. Thomas. She was a real bitch she would go through my packages take each item inspect it like a K9 throw out what she claimed I couldn't have and be disrespectful with her mouth as she did it. She wouldn't even let me put the items on the shelves to return to my peoples on the next visit. She started to make me think that her attitude towards me had nothing to do with my packages that shit was personal. Ms. Thomas was good friends with Ms. Robin, she might had been jealous of my relationship or she might have wanted a relationship of her own, shit I don't know all I know is that woman was the devil. My time at Taconic was quickly coming to an end. I couldn't wait till the day I walked out of that gate. One thing for sure I was not the same man I was when I went in. I had grown and learned so much about myself during my incarceration that sometimes I didn't recognize myself. The lesson outweighed the hardship, and I was ready to come home. When all of my peoples walked me to the gate, I became saddened about having to leave them there, but it was my turn to go. I gave them each a pound then went to the receiving room to get ready. My heart skipped a beat when I saw a brown paper bag on the shelves with my name written across the top. The day had finally arrived, and I was petrified I was so frightened of the unknown that I couldn't move. I took several deep breathe lowered my head and said a silent prayer. For the past four years I had made the prison system my home it was the first time in my life that I was secure. I knew the routine, I knew where I was going to lay my head at night and I always knew that I wasn't going to go hungry, for the first time in my life I was in control. After that day I had no clue where what or how I would survive the streets of Harlem.

The officer saw that I was in deep thought he gave me a few minutes to get myself together then handed the bag to me. He pointed towards a private room and told me to go in there to get dressed. I had asked Aunt Mary to purchase a three-piece suit and a pair of shoes. A three-piece suit is a sign that a man is making a comeback. The suit fit me perfectly I looked really dapper in that piece, but when I went to put on my shoes, I couldn't get my foot in them. I knew I specifically told her that I was a ten and a half but when I looked at the sole, Aunt Mary God bless her soul, had bought the wrong size. I wasn't even mad at her she was all I had that was solid in my life so I squeezed my foot into those shoes and made my way to the front gate I saw aunt Mary standing on the other side with her arms wide open. The officers buzzed me out I walked directly to her with my heart in my hand I hugged her and told her

"Come on mom Sammy O is Home."

CHAPTER 19

NO PLACE LIKE HOME

H arlem had gone through a complete drug overhaul while I was away. It was 1984 and as I got off the train at the Metro North station on 125th Street I noticed that the drug addicts who were loitering in the lobby were going through an ugly transition.

I took Aunt Mary by her elbow and walked her out onto street away from the dope fiends. These fiends were different for sure. Anyone could see that there was something going on with them they were not just indulging in heroin anymore, 125th St. had history and now 125th St. looked like a battle field with drug users and the dealers that allowed their neighborhood to get so bad.

Harlem was built on culture and the souls of African American families who moved into the area in the early 1900's almost every small business was owned by a black entrepreneur and I could feel the history all around me as I made my way to Lenox Ave. Although I knew the original history of Harlem, I was more drawn to the Harlem I was living in now. All of my street smarts kicked in when I got closer to my block. Aunt Mary had moved out of the apartment on 111th and into a new one on 112th. It really didn't make much of a difference to me as long as we were in the same area.

By the time I made my way to the apartment my feet were killing me the first thing I needed to do was get some money so I could get some new shoes. The wheels in my head were turning. Aunt Mary knew me, she must have seen it in my face because she made a statement that I could never forget.

"Sam, I don't want to die and you're in prison."

Those words threw me for a loop it touched me to know that even though she had been hard on me she cared about me. We made our way into the building; at that point I couldn't take it anymore I had to slip those shoes off my feet and expand my toes. I walked the rest of the way barefooted, once I entered the apartment Homer rushed over to me and hugged me it felt good to know that I was missed. The worst thing in the world is when a nigga come home, and his people don't really want him there. My family didn't have much to offer but the little they had I was welcome to it. When Homer noticed that I had my shoes in my hand he asked me what happen Aunt Mary quickly explained that she had bought me the wrong size Homer dug into his pocket passed me a few dollars and told me to get some sneakers.

It was the little things that mattered, to know that he really didn't have it like that and to still want to look out for me was dope.

Janine called me and told me that she was on her way to the house. Janine was from the Bronx she lived with her mother on 169th St. off of Morris Avenue so she didn't have a long commute. I went into the room aunt Mary had set up for me changed out of my suit and into some sweats tank top and some slippers that was laying around the house. I wasn't worried about trying to go out to shop for some footwear after four years of being locked up, all I wanted to do was to lay up with Janine and fuck. I was itching to go the block and check out the scene but that would have to wait too. I had plenty of time to get reacquainted with the hood. I did go out to the stoop to wait for Janine though, I wanted her to see what she was about to get into. My dumb ass opened the front door to 242 w 112th St. and froze my ass. It was cold as shit outside so my plans of show off my physic went down the drain. Aunt Mary had given me a pass that day she told me that she didn't want women in and out her house, so I had to take full advantage of that one-shot deal.

Janine had finally arrived, and I have to say that she was bad she was shaped like a coca cola bottle had short hair always styled in finger waves and she dressed fly. Let's not forget that she always smelled good too. I was definitely looking forward to getting my hands on her. We went into the bedroom I shut the door behind us and the rest was history. At first, I was a little rough around the edges but after a few rounds Janine was hooked. I had to admit that I was hooked too but hooked or not I was young, and I didn't want to be tied down to just one woman.

Janine left that evening with her heart on her sleeve and as soon as she walked out the door the house phone rang. Ms. Robin the officer from Taconic was on the other end talking about how she needed to see me, there is a big difference between a person wanting to see you and needing to see you.

Never in a million years did I think she would keep her word about getting together on the outside. I was all in, yet I played a little head game with her when I told her

"If you want to see me you have to wear your uniform."

She already knew what it was. While at Taconic she took every opportunity to entice me, flirt with me and challenge my manhood now she was on my turf and I was going to show her who was really in control, I was power tripping.

Early the next morning she showed up on the block to scoop me up. Robin had the whole day planned out for us and I was alright with that. It's not like I had anything else to do, anyway.

She took me on a shopping spree on 125th street, we went to get something to eat then we headed out of the city. I don't remember where we were going, and I didn't ask either. All I know is that she drove for about a forty-five minutes while I thought about all those nights at Taconic I would jerk off in her name and fantasize about putting all those babies up in her. I was mentally preparing myself you do her dirty.

The hotel was right off the highway my excitement grew as she pulled into the parking lot got of the car and went into the hotel to get the room. Once in the room I was impressed she was setting it all out for me I know she spent a pretty penny on that room. She had also mentioned that no one was going to see us there. Ms. Robin wasn't just an officer who was violating her oath not to congregate with a convicted felon. She was also married. She started to act shy, I wasn't with it though we talked for a minute about some frivolous shit then I turned into a beast I came out and told her that I want to fuck and to go put on her uniform. She went into the bathroom with her bag, I could tell that she wanted me too, but she just didn't know how to react to my aggression.

I could have fucked her at the prison if I really wanted to, but no amount of ass was going to snatch my CR date. One thing about me is that I had patience. I'm not one to jump out the window over momentary desires. But now that I had her in the position I wanted. I took complete ownership of the situation. Ms. Robin was more than worth the wait there was a lot of chemistry between us. We vibed!

Several hours later she dropped me off and pulled off from the curb with a big smile on her face. I walked away whispering

"Mission accomplished." To myself.

Life is crazy because even though I was able to get with these two women there was one woman I couldn't get out my system. Thomasina was heavy on my mind I couldn't get over what she had done to me. I waited a few days while I gathered my thoughts together before I reached out. I wasn't sure how I was going to go about it. So, it took me a minute to call my cousin Mark. Aunt Gwen answered the phone on the first ring she was so excited to hear my voice she asked me a million question and although I didn't want to be disrespectful towards her, I cut off and asked her for Mark. He was really apprehensive about getting on the phone with me. I could tell because my aunt had to call out to him a few times. When he got on the line I got straight to the point.

"Where is Thomasina?"

Mark was quick to tell me that he didn't know and that he had no relationship with her. I listened to him because I needed to know why he had betrayed me the way that he did. He went on to tell me that he never had any intentions of being with her, it was just a fuck thing. He thought that his confession was going to make me feel better, it didn't. Mark only had Thomasina's sister phone number. After I jotted the number down, I hung up. My next phone call was to Ann it felt good talking to her but like my aunt Gwen, I cut her off. I asked her about her sister I told her that I wanted to go see her and she told me to come down. Ann was always cool so when she extended the invitation, I took it

The Amtrak station in midtown was crowned I had to stand on a line to purchase my ticket to Atlanta Georgia for about 30 minutes but once I had my ticket in my hand, I made my way towards the tracks. That ride was an emotional roller coaster for 15 hours all I thought about was what I would find when I arrived. I thought about how I would feel once I seen Thomasina again. A part of me regretted getting on that train and the other part needed to. I was not going to be able to move on with my life until I came face to face with the one person, I trusted and crossed me.

Once I arrived in Atlanta, I took a cab over to Ann's house right behind me was Black Leroy. They were both happy to see me, but they were leery too. I didn't blame them for being a little intimidated because I didn't look the same, I was one hundred and twenty nine pounds that last time they saw me, now I was two hundred and twenty pounds solid, I wasted no time in getting reacquainted with them but to be honest I was there for one reason and one reason only. Ann walked into the house and called Thomasina to let her know that I was there. I'm sure Ann had told her that I was on my way I was also sure that she didn't believe it.

116

When we drove up to Thomasina's house, I was really disappointed to find her living in an old, dilapidated house, the shit was leaning to one side the result that the foundation did not settle right. The trash cans were full to the top with trash and the street was dirty. The kids who ran up and down the street was barefooted that scene was real country and that is putting it mildly. Thomasina walked to the door and invited us in I couldn't believe my eye Thomasina looked run down and drained although it looked like she tried to clean herself up and look cute, it didn't work. Time sure can change a person especially when they don't care of themselves, I thought that she only had one kid it turned out that she had three from three baby daddies. The first one being my cousin Mark second one being railroad track Aubrey and only God knows who the third was. I wanted to dog her ass out so bad, make her feel what I felt all those years but there was no point in doing that, because she ended up tormenting herself. I walked away from that situation relieved to find out that she wasn't doing better without me like I thought.

CHAPTER 20

WILLIE'S

One of the best ways to reinvent yourself is to find something that interest you and jump right in. This is where I was at after facing my past head on. Now I had to find my own way without depending on old memories and the system, being home had become one of my biggest fears. Prison had become a safe haven for me. I know that may sound strange but it's the truth. Mark my words when I say that I was institutionalized, after years of being locked up a person could become immune to a routine while being there. There were so many things I wanted to do but I had no idea how to begin. I had no formal education, the prison system handed me a one-way ticket, forty dollars and threw me out to the streets. All I knew was that I had to make money stay out of jail and be successful in anything I choose to do. Living at Aunt Mary house was alright but after a while I was getting on her nervous and she made it known that how I was behaving wasn't normal. I was waking up early to go nowhere, I broke all of her dishes by tossing them in the sink hard like I did in prison. She would really get pissed off when she would look for a fork and they weren't any because I was throwing them in the garbage.

Also, Homer was still working and like she uses to tell me as a little boy "If my man has to get up to go to work so do you." I couldn't even get mad about that because like I said I was up at the crack of dawn anyway. One morning I made my way around the corner to 111th street, it was time to show my face on the block and let everyone see the new me. I wasn't that young boy who stood on the sidelines asking to be put in the game. Sammy O already knew what he had to offer; the game was the same it was the players that changed. In order for me to make some quick bread I had to see who was out there playing ball. To my surprise half of the brothers I grew up with were either locked up or dead. When I turned that corner onto 7th Ave, I gazed up the block and that shit was empty, there was no one out there. Suddenly, I had decided to go straight to Loray's which was now owned by Willie the owner of the legendary Willie Burgers in Harlem. Loray's now named Willie's was legendary too. Willie was standing outside when I rolled up on him, he was happy to see the kid he embraced me like I was one of his own we joked, laughed and talked about how I was ready to do my thing. I even lowered myself to the ground and did a quick hundred push-ups for him. He was semi impressed with me he made it clear though that my hunger wasn't going to last long. His next statement is what really motivated me to prove myself to him.

"Come see me in three weeks and let's see if you can do those hundred push-ups again. Here's twenty dollars I can't give you anymore because then you will not want to hustle."

119

In that moment I thought he was trying to be funny towards me, like what I can I do with twenty dollars? I stood there for a few minutes until the words registered. I was determined to get on by any means necessary.

I refused to be a nobody now that I was home. Prison gave me a rep everyone knew who I was and the power I possessed I was able to move mountains. All I needed to do was to instill the same attitude I had in there out on the streets. That's when I started making my rounds, I walked back uptown in search of my childhood friend Dougie Lime we were both the same age but he was my idol. He was the first little nigga that was getting paid out of our age group. He came out of 144th St. between 7th and Lenox and I was on my way there to touch base with him. Before I hit the corner, I saw L.A. another brother that was getting major paper. I told him that I was just coming home and to look out for a brother he told me that he didn't have any money on him that he was making a move and for me to come back in a couple of days that he would have something for me. He also told me that Dougie was locked up.

I never went back because I really didn't have any money to move around but when I was about to go see him again, I heard he had been murdered. That shit hurt me to my heart because he was a good motherfucker, I wasn't able to attend his funeral either because I didn't have anything to wear and I didn't want to out like that.

Things for me was at a standstill it was now one month after my release and I found myself back where I was before I went away. There was no money coming in not even for the basic things like clothes shoes I didn't have money for food, shit was tight. The worst thing in the world is having to wear the same suit Aunt Mary bought me a hundred different ways. That's when I started staying with Janine, I had to get out of Aunt Mary house because she began to nag the shit out of me. She would get that drink in her and her voice would become squeaky like a cartoon character. Aunt Mary would start calling me a junky like she uses to. I was passed all that bullshit I was a tick tick boom so before I disrespected her, I had to move out. She wasn't wrong though when she said I needed to do something with my life, so I did. I got the fuck out!

The honeymoon with Janine was in full affect she treated me like a king. That was before I knew how a king was supposed to be treated. Her mother was cool with me staying there and to be honest the woman tried to help me get my life in order. She even went as far as speaking to a friend of hers about giving me a job. That job was at a gas station pumping gas although I didn't like the job, I was doing my thing for about a week, then I quit.

Janine's mom was pissed off at me for that so you can imagine what happen next. She complained about me to her daughter claiming that she needed her space that she couldn't walk around her house the way she wanted too. So after six months she asked me to leave, thank god that I always had a home with aunt Mary who now lived on 123rd and 124th on 7th Ave. Aunt Mary had applied for a new building that was coming up and she was called, Ennis Frances was a nice place and it was still in the hood making it convenient for all of us.

About two weeks after moving back in with my aunt I got up early, her rules, and headed towards 111th St. it must had been my lucky day because I ran into Slim who was Willie's lieutenant and also the new owner of Willies now named Charlene's after his daughter. Willie was a blessing to many people who worked for him and if you were loyal, he took care of you. Slim was unloading some supply for his spot when he noticed me and asked me to grab a box.

I helped him with no questions asked guess I had to thank Aunt Mary for making me get up and get out that day, because from that day forward I become a strong influence in Harlem.

When I walked into Charlene's Slim called me to kitchen area he went in the freezer and came out with a brown paper bag he placed it on the counter then pulled out a clear plastic bag of vials filled with a white sub. He then looks at me and says

"Boy I don't know what the fuck this shit is, but it got these motherfuckers going crazy. When they take a hit of this that shit makes them come right back. I am making a lot of money but I need help I have little Johnny Jetter working for me on the day shift but I need someone to work in the evening."

That was my cue, my time to shine and I did I took that job gladly and started hustling that evening. He already had a spot set up in the building next door to Charlene's all I had to do was relieve Johnny. My first night was hectic I had to service the custys and be my own outlook but that changed quickly when Ms. Jimmy from the first floor started to help me out, she was about sixty something years old, big old fat woman who sat at her window playing the role tenement parole.

Slim was giving me twenty-dollar vials of crack for seventeen dollars and I sold seventeen hundred vials making fifty one hundred dollar profit in one night after that I   was hooked.

Slim had created a monster, or did he?

To be honest the way I was pulling in that flow I wasn't created I was born that way. I became a beast, there wasn't enough hours in the day for me to make money.

My hunger lead to action, action lead to success.

CHAPTER 21

JEWELS

I f you don't have nothing to live for find something to die for, I had both. I lived for the almighty dollar and I was willing to die for it. Back in those days the O.G's lived by those statements which were built on philosophies those are what we call in this day and age, jewels.

I lived by those jewels, because of them I was able to bypass a lot of the bullshit I seen some of the other players go through. It was rare when you found someone who you could depend on but most importantly someone you could trust in that line of work.

I knew I was reckless at times, but I also knew that God took care of babies and fools.

I moved up in the game quickly I went from selling hand to hand in the building to hiring someone else to do that job for only seven hundred dollars a week plus spread out money. No one was going to have my back and no one was going to chase that paper like me. So, I stood outside watched out for the police and steered customers in his direction. Being that it was my first time getting some real money and, in the speed, that I was getting it I went through a few set-backs.

Joe Grant's gambling spot was down the block on 111th St. and 112th on Saint Nick. It reminded me of a private social club for members only. I remember the place from when I was growing up. I overheard some of the guys on the block talking about they were going over there to gamble tonight. Now that I was hustling and getting a couple of dollars, I decided to make my way to the spot and try my luck. I set everything up with my worker told him that if he needed anything to beep me. I made my ways to spot with a little over fifteen hundred dollars in my pocket by the time I left I was broke. There was a female by the name of Carol from 114th St. who got her skills from her father Calvin aka Twenty, a big-time gambler from Harlem, so the apple didn't fall far from the tree. She cracked (beat) my ass so quick and sent me up out of there. I walked back to my spot licked my wounds and finished off my shift.

Slim was suppling me with so much work that I had to get myself a place in the neighborhood to stash the work.

Sam Jr. was in my life although we weren't that close, we still tried to maintain some type of relationship. He was now living with his new girl and her son on 111th on Manhattan Ave. I went over to see him a few times and while there one day I told him that I need to find a room. His girl overheard me then told me that she had an extra room and that she was willing to rent out for one hundred and fifty dollars a week. In my opinion I couldn't think of a better place. I would have my own where I was free to do what I wanted to do. And who better to have my back then my pops. Little did I know that renting that room would cost me my relationship with Slim.

At first the room was supposed to be my stash house but once I found myself spending a lot of time there, I decided to hook up the space for myself with a brand-new queen-size bed, T.V. lounge chair and a stereo. It was the first time in my life that I really had my own, so I went all out.

It was a Friday night and I was hanging out on the block when I saw this pretty light skin girl coming out of the corner store. I couldn't help myself when I started to flirt with her, I asked for her name told her how I wanted to get to know her better, etc. Tangie was all for it she stared me up and down took a pen out her bag and jotted down my beeper number and left. As she walked away, I yelled out to her "Don't forget to call me."

The rest of the evening was going smoothly I opened up shop at midnight my worker was on point like always and I of course was standing outside when all of a sudden Slim pulled up walked directly to me and asked me

"What the fuck is this?." as he handed me two vials. I took one look at them and said, "Those are your bottles."

He was in a rage and I didn't know why I was completely clueless. It turned out that some of the customers were complaining about the work. However, that was putting it lightly the customers were going directly to Slim with the product and the product turned out to be Rice Krispies.

Since Slim was the only one who bottled his own work there was no way that the bottles could have been dummies unless I the one who was responsible for them, made them that way.

I might had been only twenty-one but I was a man of integrity and I wasn't about to cut my own throat; besides, I was making too much money for that. I wasn't going to scarify my position on Slims crew for twenty or thirty dollars. There had to be a logical explanation either Slim was trying to play me or someone else, but until I could find out what was going on Slim stopped trusting me. I had to pay Slim all of the money back for the dummies that were turn in to him which set me back. I even went as far as going uptown to the Dominicans buy there ten-dollar vials and then come back to the block to sell it for twenty dollars. That didn't fly with the customers because the work was trash.

I was on prowl I was going to find out what the hell happen to my work one day while sitting in the room I looked up towards the ceiling, above the door there was a window with a small latch on it. The window didn't look out to the street it was one of those that looked out into the apartment's hallway. Then it hit me someone was crawling through that space and into the room. They were switching the vials on me. I got up opened the door looked up from the other side and there it was I seen a gap. Then I headed for the kitchen opened up the cabinet to see what was inside I wasn't surprised when I found an open box of Rice Krispies.

CHAPTER 22

WIRED DIFFERENT

If life hadn't kicked me in the ass so many times, I would have never made the moves I made. No one knew that when I had made that first five-thousand dollars. I had gone to Janine and told her to get us an apartment. I was learning to cover my ass no matter what, I was also learning not to let your left hand know what your right hand was doing. That was the smartest move I had made because after I confronted my pop, his girl and her son I knew I had to get the work out of there eventually.

I went to work my shift that night with a heavy heart, it took all of me not to catch a body. Someone in that house fucked me over and I would never find out who did it but I had an idea. There was no need for my pops to steal from me and his girl was satisfied with me paying my rent and hitting her off from time to time with a few extra dollars. It had to be her grimy ass son who would wait for me to leave, make sure my pops and his moms were asleep then make his way into my space to do me dirty.

Before I arrived on the block, I had to change my attitude quickly there was no more room for mistakes. I had to make that bread and make things right with Slim. As I turned the corner onto 7th Ave, I noticed a new guy by the name of Love standing in the building and my worker standing outside. I went straight into Charlene's to talk to Slim. Before I was able to approach him, he raised his hand as though to stop me. I asked him what the fuck was going on, I was not going to let his hand gesture stop me from getting clarity, up until the dummy situation Slim and I had built a friendship. And to see someone else out there holding down my position bothered me. Slim made it clear that he had replaced me because he didn't trust me anymore, he went on to tell me that it wasn't personal it was strictly business. That shit broke my heart because I was on the up and up and for him to see me as a snake offend me. He had the power to shut me down and he did. Now I found myself with no work no spot and no money. That is when I learned that if I would have saved money, money would have saved me.

As fast as I made the money, I spent it. Not once did I think about saving for a rainy day. I also had developed a gambling habit. I went to the Joe Grants almost every night, thinking if I lost any money, I would be able to make it up the next day, I was wrong.

But I was wired different although I went through all the basic betrayals in such a short time. I was not going to allow that experience to define me.

Back at my pop place I went straight into my room grabbed my T.V. and stereo then I jumped into a cab and headed to the Bronx.

It was strange entering my apartment I had spent so much time in Harlem that I never really got the chance to enjoy my place with Janine. If nothing else I did make sure that the apartment was fully furnished rent was paid up to date and there was food in the refrigerator. I set my things by the door and walked into the bedroom where Janine was sleeping, I tried to be quiet when I stood over her, Janine was a good woman, she attended college classes and worked at a D'Agostino supermarket somewhere in Manhattan. I took off my clothes climbed into the bed next to her and took a deep breath, she stirred and laid her head on my chest. I don't know why I hadn't done that sooner. I asked myself while I laid there in thought. Guess I needed that comfort at the time. I wasn't one of those men who laid around and played house. I had already had a taste of the street life and just because Slim had cut me off didn't mean that I was going to bow down. The thought of getting comfortable at the crib was not acceptable. I had a deep hunger for money that no woman could fulfill. That visit only lasted but so long.

Two days later I was back at Charlene's if you wanted to get money you had to be around money. You never knew who you would run into if you were at the right place at the right time. That saying was true for me because while there my homegirl Robin walked into Charlene looking for me. She had been looking for me for a few days, she told me that she was living at a welfare hotel on 28th St. and that there was a lot of money to be made. Robin described the set up and how everyone down there was smoking crack she went on to tell me that the only thing that was missing was the work. She even offered me her room to work out for a fee of course. Robin wanted me to go down there to check it out but what was the point if I didn't have the supply to feed the masses.

I was on it though, if it was anything like she said it was I was not going to pass up on the opportunity.

That night I decided to go over to Tangie house on 116th on St Nick. I had to stay in the hood in order to make some moves in the morning. But before I made my way into the building, I was surprised to find that the building was completely abandoned. The building was dim the paint was chipping from the walls the elevator was not working. I walked up the steps to her apartment and knocked on the door I heard her talking to someone so I knew she wasn't alone, once inside I was pleasantly surprised to find that her apartment was nice. She introduced me to her mother sister and the sister's boyfriend Lamont who became one of my closet friends and eventually my worker. I stayed there for about a week until I got in touch with my cousin Gums. I told him my situation, he told me he had no Coke but that he would introduce me to someone who did. He introduced to a player that everyone called Uncle Wayne, he never came through with the product although he told me he would. I had to go back to my cousin Gums and tell him that Uncle Wayne wasn't about business and I need something now in order to get that spot popping.

That's when Gums set up an introduction between Quarterfield and me.

I had finally got the call from Gums telling asking me to stay where I was because he was sending someone down to talk to me.

I was on 111th and 7th Ave doing some pull ups, in order to keep my mind right I had to work out on a daily basis. My stress level was on over drive and working out kept me balanced.

Quarterfield pulled up with Guy Woods founder of 5001 Flavors.

They pulled up in a white civic all pimped out with rims, sheep skin seats and a bombing system. They both got out he car and did a thorough inspection of me Quarterfield introduced himself with confidence told me that he had heard good things about me from Gums and that he was ready do some business. I told me about the hotel and all the money we were going to make as long as he could keep up with the supply. We started with a deal of 70/30 split 70% went to him 30% to me. I wasn't worried about the split at the time I just wanted to get the spot up and running. I knew that eventually I was going to come back to the table to renegotiate the numbers. But until then I was good.

After I made that deal with Quarterfield Wayne showed up two days later with two kilos talking about, I got it for you. When I told him that I had already hooked up with Quarterfield he knew he had lost out. I couldn't wait around for someone to get the work I needed someone who already had it.

That same night I went down to the hotel opened shop and made so much money that Quarterfield couldn't keep up with the demand. He had to create a system that worked for the both of us. Being that it was our first night we did the best we could with what we had but at the end of the day I walked out of there paid.

I ran into a few hiccups the first couple of days, but like any other business some things had to be revamped.

CHAPTER 23

THE SYSTEM

R evamping a business takes skills the first thing I had to do was cancel my arrangement with Robin it turned out that when Robin offered her room for me to work out of she never discussed it with her husband, not only was he upset about having the whole building, and then some, knocking on his door. He was upset at the way Robin catered to my every need. There wasn't anything that I didn't need that she did not provide. So, I can see where he was not happy with the arrangement. The second thing I had to do was get help I wanted to have the spot open twenty-four hours a day, I needed someone to work the morning shift. Since, staying at Tangie's Lamont and I had become very close it was rare that I made a move and he wasn't right there next to me. I offered him the position and he accepted. The third thing I had to do was have a sit down with Quarterfield and Guy we had to come up with a plan as to how we were going to get the work downtown in a timely matter. There was no way that I would let the well run dry. Guy was the one who would be bringing the work to me and if he wasn't available Quarterfield gave me his word that he would have someone else bring it down.

It was my third night at the hotel, I walked into Robin's room with Lamont and from the door I felt the negative vibes, Robin's husband was not having it. He was definitely feeling some type a way about me you could see it all over his face. To be honest I didn't blame him because if I had to go through my woman to get some bread, I would be feeling some type of way too. I had already made up my mind about getting another room to work out of so his attitude towards me was irrelevant. I wasn't there for that bullshit I was only there to get money. With that in mind I collected my bread left her with what was left over from the day shift to finish off. I went straight to security put him on the payroll after I had a few words with him my motto was and will always be that everybody had to eat. He was the one that put me on to a couple who shared a room on the fifth floor so I opened up shop there and then he hooked me up with a vacant room for me and Lamont that we worked out of too. We were only three day in and already I had three rooms open for business. The word spread quickly amongst the crack addicts inside the hotel and out on the street.

More money more problems that's what they say however that was not the case when it came to me and my business, expanding was. But until I was able to do that, I was enjoying my success. I bought my first car a black on black BMW 325i coupe that Quarterfield showed me how to pimp out, we went and got pipping seats, rims and a mean stereo system. I began to shop at A.J. Lester's where a met a sale girl who became my personal stylist she even went as far as telling me to go buy

Playboys and British Walkers to match my outfits. She noticed that whenever I went by the store I was always squinting, she asked me if I needed glasses and of course I was honest with her. I explained to her that I hated to wear glasses, that's when I discovered contact lenses. Those contact lenses changed my life I didn't feel awkward anymore and the best part of it was that I was able to see, for years I had been walking around Harlem blind.

Everything I ever wanted in life was now my reality thank God that I was able to handle the come up I had BOSSED UP and I was enjoying my life, finally. I had my crew running the hotel I had Quarterfield suppling the drugs and now I had females all over my body. Can you imagine that nappy headed boy with the thick glass who once was overlooked was now getting more pussy then the law allowed?

Strength was in the numbers and the numbers never lied. The work was being sold so fast that at the welfare hotel that Quarterfield couldn't keep up with the demand. I started falling back a little from being at the hotel because I was back in Harlem enjoying my new found wealth, or what I thought was wealth. Lamont was holding the spot down like a true hustler, the trust factor was never questioned between us he always had my money correct down to the very last cent. This is why when I went down to the hotel one day to pick up some money, I was hurt to find out that Lamont had started smoking crack. When I tried to enter the room, he had the chain on the door like normal it was how long it took him to open the door that tweeted my curiosity. I knew that something was wrong because he had never done that before. When he finally opened the door, I did a quick survey of the room and found some crack paraphernalia sitting on the end table by the bed.

He was high but when I walked in, he tried to straight up. Also, the fact that he hasn't been home in a few days his clothes was in shambles his hyenine was not up to par and that was not the Lamont I knew. So, I just straight up asked me if he was getting high and he turned to me and told me the truth. He stated that "I left him down there by himself, I thought we was a team I got caught up with one of these bitches and now I don't know how to get myself out."

That shit hurt me to my heart Lamont was my boy and now we were headed in different directions. I had on a button up sweater with my name written across its Sammy O I was so heated that I took it off hung it behind a chair then went to clear my mind. When I returned to the building, I got in the elevator with three other individuals. They looked like crackheads but there was something strange about them, when they pressed the button for the tenth floor something told me to press nine. You know Geminis have a sixth sense and on that day my gut told me that something was going to go down. Lamont got arrested along with two other people that insisted Lamont serve them. While I was lurking on the ninth floor, I overheard all of the commotion. I was concerned for Lamont but I was more worried about them finding my sweater and putting two and two together. Lamont was irreplaceable but I had to keep the spot going so I had to find a new worker, there was always someone ready to get that paper. A few days after that Guy who drove from Harlem to the hotel with fifteen vials of crack two or three times a day, showed up at the spot shook, he expressed to me that he was not going to make those runs anymore. I asked him what he was going to do and he said, "I'm going to make clothes." I found that strange because I always thought that women were the one who made clothes.

Guess he proved me wrong because look how successful he is now. He is the owner of the 5001 flavors clothing co and the store owner of Harlem Haberdashery Boutique.

Now was the time to expand my operation.

I had to start looking for another connect to fill my orders. My vision was not limited to the hotel I wanted to expand my business. That was when I lucked up and ran into Bobby at Charlene. Bobby had been bringing back kilos of cocaine from the islands and distributing them throughout the hood. Lucky for me my status for getting money was spreading fast, my hunger for the game was spreading fast too. Although I was humble in many ways, I was also very aggressive about mine. I was not about to take any loses, I knew all too well what taken a lost could mean. It would mean that I could easily go back to where I was, broke.

Guess when Bobby heard that I was looking for a new connect he offered his services to me; he even went as far as to share his connect from the Bahamas. He told me that if I wanted to make some real money, I had to get the work at a reasonable price then come back and sell it for more. I already had the calculation in my head when he said that he was going to give me the keys for nine thousand a pop. He gave me one on consignment it only took two days to pay that off. What I did was I put the word out that I had weight now. I sold half for ten thousand got his money out the way and the other half I broke it down and put it in my spot. And I was off to the races after that, I had never seen so much money like that in my life. You have to understand that with every flip I was setting a new goal for myself. Because I came from nothing people underestimated me, they didn't see it coming and with success I had to learn to act as though I had always been there.

CHAPTER 24

THE COME UP

The day had finally arrived that I would be making my first trip out to the Bahamas. Bobby had made all of the arrangements and told me to just pack a small bag. It was simple for him to purchase the tickets set up a rental and a hotel room for our stay. He mastered his travels back and forth from his hometown, unlike me who had never been nowhere outside of the United States. I was now twenty-two years old and, on a hold, different level. There was no turning back from this move and like I said earlier Harlem didn't see it coming. How I was coming out with this move was going to be legendary.

Dollar signs danced around in my head as I went over to Janine's to one pack a bag and two to let her know that I was going out of town. She wasn't too happy about that but it was what it was. Nothing or no one was going to discourage me from doing what I had to do to get where I wanted to go.

I was on a mission.

Bobby and I arrived at JFK got out of the cab grabbed our bags and headed towards the check in booth.

I stood there for a few second in awe as I walked towards a window that faced the landing strip the airplanes were departing and landing into the airplane, I was excited. There was no way for me to know what to expect when we got to the Bahamas but again, I had to act as those I had been there. We boarded the plane, waited a few minutes for take-off and in no time, we were up in the air my stomached flipped my ears popped but outside of that the trip was smooth.

The trip to the Bahamas was about 2 hrs. 47 min long, when we arrived, we landed at the Grand Bahama International Airport as I got off the plane the clean crisp air hit my face abruptly. That type of breeze hits different when you're coming from Harlem where the air was filled with pollution. I was so used to that environment that when I felt what the islands had to offer, I recognized it immediately. We went to pick up our rental and drove about fifteen minutes into a small town. The streets in that town was filled with rubble the villagers were dressed in shorts t shirts and some were even barefooted. I could tell that it was a poor little town filled with poverty but the way that the kids ran up to the car as we drove down the road slowly, it was also filled with hustlers.

The homes were built from wood, straw and clay I noticed an older male gentleman rocking in his chair carving a sugar cane, while an older female washed clothes in a steal pale. Bobby stopped the car in front of some kids got out of and started to talk to them. Because the steering wheel was on the right side of the vehicle, I had to lean over to hear what he was saying.

I heard a young boy no older than about eleven or twelve tell him.

"I got two" and then another young boy tells him "I got one". Bobby asked them how much and they both said three thousand American dollars. That whole transition with these small kids was all new to me. I couldn't believe how in the Bahamas there was such freedom in which the islanders were allowing their kids to sell cocaine so freely. Although I was new to all of that I wasn't new to the numbers. Bobby was getting the kilos for three thousand then wanted to sell them to me for nine thousand which was at the lower end because he was selling it to everyone else for thirteen dollars making a ten-dollar profit.

Drug trafficking was at an all-time high on the islands and the Drugs dealers from the states found ways to get those drugs from Latina America and into their communities quickly creating Drug Kingpins, for me to find myself in that situation was priceless. Bobby intentions was to get about fifteen kilos his motto was that all of the money he brought to the island was not going back. He gathered whatever they had on hand and walked back to the car. Later on, that evening he went back to get the rest.

I was curious to know how these kids were getting that work, so I asked Bobby as we drove to another section of the island this section being a whole lot nicer. Bobby told me that they would go out in the evening wait by the beach for the Colombians to drop shipments into the water, they would quickly jump in swim out to meet the crates that were filled with hundreds of kilos, grab whatever they could get their hands on go back to their town and sell it. They had a whole system going on that nine times out of ten it worked. The only time that it didn't was when customs showed up with their boats and ceased the merchandise.

We pulled up to a liquor store Bobby asked for fifteen bottles of Bohemian Rum that was packaged in a dark brown bottle. Again, I became curious fifteen kilos and fifteen bottles something was up. Bobby was somewhat secretive in the hood, yet he was exposing me to all his business on the island. I wondered why he had chosen me to share it with. I was already getting restless, I wanted to go the hotel to rest, change my clothes and hopefully hit the town. I expressed this to Bobby and he drove us straight to a small building he parked the car and told me to follow him. The whole time we were there I thought that we were going to stay at a hotel it turned out that Bobby had a two-bedroom condo out there. We walked into the apartment and it was something out of a magazine. The man had great taste you can tell from the décor and he had spent a lot of money on the plush sofa set he had sitting in the middle of the living room the wall to wall carpeting the bar among all of the other things that filled the room not that to mention the bedrooms that were fully furnished in luxury. I felt like a king, a young nigga from Harlem who slept in movie theaters and stole money in order to eat could easily get used to living like that.

Later that evening Bobby went out to pick up the other eight kilos, upon his return he locked himself into his bedroom. When he finally came out a few hours later he had the brown bottles he purchased at the liquor store filled with liquid cocaine sealed and ready for delivery. He stated that they were gifts for family and friends he was bringing back to the states from his vacation. Several days later we were back on the streets of Harlem he took his work did what he had to do, me I refused to pay nine thousand for a kilo of cocaine now that I knew he only paid three thousand. I walked away from that deal a winner I got the plug the resources and I only payed the three thousand apiece for five kilos. If that wasn't a come up, I don't know what is. Now that I was selling weight, I didn't have to deal with the welfare hotel it was time to explore other territories.

CHAPTER 25

MOMMY ISSUES

J anine was still in the picture although I was never around, she held on to what she thought we had, she was my security blanket everything that I wasn't. Throughout all of my craziness she maintained the house her job and her studies, she was wifey material for sure she cooked, cleaned did laundry you name it she did everything she had to do to make a nigga comfortable. That's why I had to make her my first stop to drop off some money. If it was at another place in time, I might had settled down with her. Stayed faithful and the whole nine yards. However, that is not what I wanted at the time I had missed out on so much in my life that now that I had everything I ever dreamed of; I was going to live. She was getting tired of our living arrangement so eventually she started hanging out and that is when she caught my future wife Starr with my chain on at Skate Key in the Bronx. She gave me an ultimatum making me choose between her and Starr, so we broke up and she moved on. It really didn't matter to me because she deserved to be happy. Don't get me wrong I appreciated everything she had done for me while my incarceration, but that was then.

Women came at me from all over Westside, Eastside, Uptown Harlem, Bronx and even New Jersey. The attention I was getting was sometimes overwhelming, The O.G.s never lied when they said once you reach a certain status in the game women stayed auditioning for a position. I was the new kid on the block so when one girl had the chance to meet me, they would tell a friend who would tell a friend. Some of these females were so desperate to be with a nigga that was paid, that they would cut their own friends throats just to get a taste of me. I treated each woman I dealt with accordingly. If you were a hoe you got treated like a hoe, if you were a lady, I treated you like one. My reaction to them was based on how they carried themselves not only in front of me but when I wasn't around. It didn't matter how good a chick looked most of them were broke and they were just looking for a come up.

However, I found myself being a gentleman towards all women that was important to me because I might not had been raised by my mother but I was raised by a mother. And if anyone dared to mistreat Aunt Mary there would have been consequences. Who was I to judge these women they were all looking for something, but so was I.

Aunt Mary loved me but there was a major element lacking in our relationship and that was affection, it was rare when she hugged me, kissed me or even said that she loved me. I'm sure that if alcohol didn't play a part of her daily life things would have been different.

I felt the same way about Beverly I tried my best to forgive her for her lack of interest in me while growing up, but it was difficult. Yes, she was caught up in the streets and so involved in her world that she had forgotten all about mine. Even after she cleaned up and we reconnected on that visit in Bedford N.Y. I still left like there was something missing. There wasn't a day that didn't go by when I was out on the streets hustling that I didn't think about her that I didn't wanted to share my wealth with her. Beverly couldn't be bothered there was always an excuse as to why she was distant but most of all cold. I would have given anything to have my mother's love, and I mean that literally. Guess this was why building connections with many different women was my way of filling a void. A void that wasn't easily filled and if it was, it didn't last very long.

Learning to master hardships and loneliness was a challenge for me however I was overcoming them by being involved with multiple women and learning from each experience.

The first was Thomasina who broke my heart by cheating on me and having a kid by my cousin.

Then there was Janine who was there for me during my incarceration but expected much more than I could give her.

Tangie who I stayed with in Harlem so that I could be close to the hood and the up rise of my drug business.

Then there was Tanya who claimed to give me my first son, we weren't in a relationship which had me doubting her claims. Nevertheless, he is my son and was named after me, Sammy O.

Then there was Elaine who gave me my 2nd child Monay, I wasn't in a relationship with Elaine either. Monay was a blessing, nevertheless.

Doreen who gave me my 3rd child Alicia she was the one who never gave up on me if she didn't hear from me for while she would find me. I married her too because she gave me an ultimatum while I was incarcerated on my second bid and I needed someone to do the time with me.

Tanya who I met at Virginia Beach but lived in Queens gave me my son Tyriq she was the first woman I called when I wanted to move to South Carolina to start a new life, she said no.

Then there was GiGi Shame's aka J.B.'s aunt, who I loved very much she also said no when I asked her to move with me.

That is when I called Starr and she stated she was going to pack up and meet me in twenty minutes, because of her loyalty Starr is who I built a relationship with and married. We moved to Goose Creek South Carolina where I purchased a mansion in the Saint James estates development. Where we lived until she was killed in the Bronx.

Then there was Lori who gave me my 5th child Shelby. I was in a relationship with her but she was crazier than a bus filled with Jerry Lewis kids, and let's not forget how when I got locked up on my 2nd bid, she had abandoned me.

Tesha who gave me my son Samson, was more like my crimey we did business together and was down for each other a lot like Bonnie & Clyde.

All of this may be a little confusing so let me clarify a few things I was with all of these women at the same time. I set the rules, if they wanted to be with me, I gave them a list of the do's, the don'ts and the better nots. The ones who followed the rules were able to stay around and reap the benefits of moving out of their situations, drive in luxury cars, wear minks and drip in the finest jewels. Those that didn't were welcomed to go back to the projects.

I loved women who were submissive they had to know how to keep a man like me. Especially if I was taking care of them and they didn't want for nothing. When I called on them, I expected them to be on point by keeping up with their appearance, keeping my home clean and their pussy wet. I was the one with the power and it was all about me. I demanded their respect, most of all I demanded that they showed me how they felt about me. I was the trophy, the prize, the one who took care of them, so it was my way or the highway. So, you see that void that I had lingering inside of me because of Beverly I passed down to all of the women that were in my life. I was told on many accusations by a few of them, that although I was treating them like queens, providing everything they ever wanted in life they were living their lives filled with loneliness. It took me a long time to understand that, wonder if Beverly ever understood that too.

These are just a few of the women I dealt with who made an impact in my life some were the first to show me what they were willing to do for me and some actually birthed life for me. I had twelve women pregnant at the same time all who wanted to be with me all who were willing to give me children if I said yes to them and made them my number one. I was still too young for all that I just got off on the power I had over them.

Power over everything in my life money tends to do that sometimes.

CHAPTER 26

THE CONNECT

How can you tell me how to make a million if you never had a million? I created the blueprint from scratch once I got back from the Bahamas and started to hit everyone off, I became the connect in Harlem I was the go-to man for the work. The difference between me and the ones who came before me was that I didn't fuck with a lot of people and I stayed out the way. My philosophy was that if the heat comes it could only be one of the two niggas I served. If you look back on the history of Harlem and the drug game when anything major happened, you will find that it was always someone that was close to them. You didn't have to look across the street, the snake would be standing right beside you, because how would the nigga across the street know intimate things about you. Like where you live where you kept your stash and the main thing, you're safe. Harlem had so many players in the 80's most were pass the million-dollar status, but for each dollar they made they made enemies. I was fully aware of these facts this is why before I left my house, I had two pockets full of money. One for myself and the other for the people I shared the wealth with. It didn't matter who they were or what they were into if someone asked me for a few dollars I always blessed them because I knew what it was to have nothing, in return those same people kept me informed.

My expansion was in motion I opened a spot on 111ᵗʰ St. in building 215 from there I opened a spot in the Bronx I even went as far as south street in Newburgh N.Y. Each spot was bringing in anywhere from thirty thousand to fifty thousand a week and that's not even counting the weight, bricks were moving at twenty-one thousand apiece but for Quarterfield who ended up coping from me was getting it for sixteen thousand due to the fact that he had put me on when I had the hotel. The money from selling the bricks was all good but I had rather kept them for myself because I made more money by breaking them down and distributing them to the spots. In my first two months of coming back from the Bahamas I had made so much money I didn't know what to do with it. I really didn't have any vices I didn't drink I didn't get high the only things that I got into was gambling, women and dressing. I have a saying that I always use to say when I was hanging out with the fellows

All I do is Rest, Dress and Fuck the Best.

I didn't need anyone to amp me up I was my own hype man, confidence, began to build a life of its own. Sammy O was now the man and no one's opinion mattered if you weren't supplying me or putting me in a position to make money you couldn't tell me shit.

There were the good times and then there were the bad, there was always one out of the bunch who would fuck shit up. I had recruited my cousin Mark, yeah, the same one who put a baby up in my first love, to work in my spot on 111th St. He eventually fucked up and started smoking and jerking my money.

In the Bronx I had recruited my other cousin Jumbo who held the stash and fed the spot whenever they were running low, he too started smoking so much so, that the costumers started to complain that the work was light. I didn't feel like I had to babysit him because I trusted him until I went to pick up a thousand grams (kilo) from the stash to serve one of my customers, when the individual went back to his place, he weighed it and it was eighty grams short. That's when I found out that Jumbo started smoking too, I was so pissed off and embarrassed with that transaction that I beat the shit out of him. What I really wanted to do was kill his ass. That ass whipping must have scared the shit out of him because he never smoked again. That type of rage was dangerous in my line of work so learning self-control was a major factor in the game. Egos brought on a constant need for praise a need to always feel superior I didn't need none of those things I had the power to change my circumstances and I had become wise enough to know that I had nothing to prove to anyone. My quest was based on making money not making enemies.

Everything was a gamble and although I had the power to take out lives, I never did. Why would I bring more heat to my situation? If something or someone didn't work out, I would take the lost and keep it moving. Let's just be clear that I had a lot of respect on the streets those small situations were done by family members not your average Joe.

This is why I don't do business with family or friends; I rather look out for them then to put their loyalty to the test.

There was enough room in Harlem for everyone to eat back in the eighties however there were some people that refuse to see things that way they became territorial mixed with violence and sometimes even death, power tripping at its finest. Because of my essential thinking process, I leveled up in all areas of my life, not only was I at the top of my game with my own business I moved on to run someone else's.

Willie Burgers on 145th and 8th Ave was famous for its Burgers sure the place was iconic and the owner was legendary for opening up several after hour clubs like the S&S Club, the Zodiac Club, Willies Lounge on 125th even a skating rink called the Rooftop, but there was more to Willie that people didn't know about. I had the honor to work with him side by side on his business ventures, here is where I started to think like an entrepreneur to run an establishment outside of my street business. Willie watched me advised me and eventually took me under his wing and made me his god son. He always reminded me about that twenty dollars he had given me and the words that he said to me stayed with me forever. Those words were the motivation I needed to get on my game, once he seen that I was about my business, he took my skills to another level.

His teachings became the foundation I needed to overcome the street life although the streets gave me all the money a man could ever want. I needed structure in order to make that money work for me. He made sure to bless me with many affirmations that would later organize my life.

Build a foundation was one of the first thing Willie told me to do. He made it clear that I had to have a home to go home to, staying in hotels with different women was not a good look. He also told me that some women were not to be trusted and that for a price they were capable of setting me up to get killed.

Move in silence, I use to have an entourage of people with me all the time Willie schooled me on how others would perceive me by the company I kept. So, I started to move around on my own.

If a man knew what you were thinking he knew how to come for you. I never told anyone anything I just marched to the beat of my own drum.

It doesn't cost you a dime to be polite, you open more doors with honey then you do with vinegar. Always smile because a smile defuses a lot of situations.

Look out for your people so they can look out for you, the people are the ones who have their ear to the streets. They will always remember how you may have taken them out of a jam and return the favor one day.

People remember the good and the bad they don't remember nothing in between.

Success is the best revenge it's not how you fall it's how you get up because I make money, money don't make me

Willie once told me that my generation was fucked up, that instead of working together as a team by respecting each other and what they represented they competed, killed each other for a title they couldn't even live up too. Some people were not built for the lifestyle yet played the game as though they could. Willie also shared with me how he wanted to fix my way of thinking before he leaves this earth. He wanted me to be successful but most importantly he wanted to show me how to be successful and be safe.

I never really understood that until he passed that torch down to me.

CHAPTER 27

S&S CLUB

C ome in peace or leave in pieces! That's what I use to say as I stood on the front lines of the S&S club. I wasn't surprised when Willie asked me to work at the club one night, he was re-evaluating his businesses and the club needed to be managed with care due to the customers that were coming through, for any business to be successful you had to move with the times or get left behind. Willie had a variety of whose who coming to hang out at the club, when he noticed that the clientele was changing, he had to revamp his establishment and hire new employees that would make sure his customers were pleased with the service but most importantly that they were safe.

That was a smart move on his part and because I knew what he was trying to instill in me, I accepted. It felt good to know that he trusted me enough to work at his club.

The S&S club was an after-hour spot which was located at 145th on 8th Ave right above Willie Burgers. There was a lot of money running through that place and Willie felt that I was ready to be on the other side of the business. I admired him for wanting to teach me how to be a businessman. The street life was temporary and there were no guarantees that I would make it into my thirties the way thing was going in Harlem.

He was a class act all on his own, but he couldn't do it on his own. He had a team that he could have easily continued to work with but for some reason he saw something in me. My strengths my views and my influence on the streets made me an asset not a liability. When he made me his private enforcer, the one who overseen his whole operation I understood the importance of the position. He was a strong male figure in my life he was the father I never had, the influence I needed in my life to show me the way. It wasn't what you did in life it's how you did it. I followed suit because I knew that under him, I would become the man I needed to be. There was still honor between men in Harlem.

My first night on the job I stood at the door smiled my million-dollar smile and made an ever-lasting impression on Willie as well as his guests. I surveyed the club's plush sleek interior as it began to get filled with nothing but money, did my rounds, said my hellos made sure that everyone had what they needed to have a good time.

The private gambling room wreaked of expensive cigars, top of the line cognac and rich cologne. There wasn't one person who sat around that gambling table playing cee-lo that didn't have hard cash at stake and I'm talking about huge amounts of money. My job was to make sure the place ran smoothly but more so that the people were comfortable. I still had a whole lot of hood in me but with time my demeanor changed because I didn't want to be king for a day, I wanted to be king forever. And with that goal in mind making a transformation was key.

All of Willies employees had their positions in place front door security, bartenders' waitresses', cleaners, me I oversaw the whole operation.

S&S was open seven days a week Monday thru Thursday was just for the individuals who wanted to gamble, Friday and Saturday nights the club was opened to everyone, there was always a line that spread around the corner, people came from all over. I had a thing about having a V.I.P. section that didn't existence at the club, because everyone was V.I.P when they stepped in the S&S no one was better than the other no matter how much money they had, that concept kept the place bumping. One thing I learned from being on the street was that with that lifestyle came a lot of responsibilities, we could become so engrossed in the business that we forget to live a little. Some people may think that just because we was making a lot money that we didn't need five minutes to feel normal, I gave them that at the club I gave everyone the chance to just sit back and relax this is why Willie and I were strict about the way we searched people at that door.

No weapons no deception!

Same concept went for the Zodiac that was also on 145th St. that spot was a lot smaller, so Willie kept it for members only. You had to be verified to get in. The lay out was different then the S&S club more intimate with a gambling table a juke box and a small bar. Cocaine spread like wildflower within the Zodiac, so we had that on lock down Willie was providing a gram of cocaine for a hundred dollars to his most prestigious clients. The spot was so private that if you went there to gamble sniff and drink no one really knew about it unless you talked about it. The isolation of the Zodiac brought out some of the biggest cee-lo players in Harlem making the place very successful.

Willie was making so much money from these afterhours that he went out and opened another bar by the name of Willie's Lounge on 125th St. This bar was open to everyone, there were no restrictions outside of what was the required by the law. There was no gambling no drug use no V.I.P section. Its was strictly a lounge with a bar and bar stools for the average person, between Willies Burgers and the all three clubs Willie was bringing in about fifty thousand a day and that was after all of his employees were paid.

That was a different type of money especially when it was under the radar, no IRS payments no audits. But no matter how secure he felt in his tax position Willie always kept a good record just in case they came after him. Because what kind of bird can't fly? A jail bird.

There were many social clubs throughout New York but the S&S club became a landmark within the community. I was so honored to have been a part of that whole experience and what I learned from my godfather was incomparable to what I had learned on the streets.

While I was getting my in-house education on running a business, Willie always reminded me to get my housing situation in order. There were no more hotel rooms for me when I signed a lease and got the keys to my second apartment. The Excelsior II was the most luxurious hi-rise building in the heart of Hackensack N.J. with a 24-hour doorman, concierge, fitness center, sauna, spa, indoor pool and private parking for my cars the amenities were endless. When I put that key in the door and turned the knob, I had an overwhelming feeling of accomplishment. I had an outstanding place to call my own now, more money than I could count and a godfather that taught me how to put my priorities in order.

Time stood still as I made my way through each room, I walked around the apartment in a zone. I couldn't believe that I was finally at a place in my life that I could be comfortable, that I didn't have to struggle to get by, I had come a long way from living in that old tenant building on 111th St.

I envisioned my younger self watching the movie Black Caesar and always wanting to live my life like Tommy Gibbs like him I had paid the cost to be the boss.

It was all up from here, I thought to myself as I walked onto the balcony looked out at the scenery raised my arms above my head and said out loud "I have made it!"

Who would have thought that I would have beat the odds?

Times were good, really good especially when a man like me had made it out the hood.

CHAPTER 28

LONELY AT THE TOP

No matter how successful you may become in life there is always something that is more important then money and that is family.

Sundays, no matter what I was doing during the week, I looked forward to Aunt Mary's dinners. It had become a tradition in her household. She was adamant about having her family and friends together under one roof. It was our time to eat laugh and talk about whatever we did during the week. Aunt Mary loved to cook for us she was always on point about bringing that southern cuisine to the north. Her mac and cheese collard greens turkey wings and my favorite sweet cornbread was the high light of my weekend, I treasured those days to the fullest. My cousins Sheila, Kathy-Ann, Janice and whatever girl I was dating at the time would show up and show out. When together we were able to relax and be ourselves, we would reminisce about the things we experienced in the past as a family and talked about our future endeavors. Aunt

Mary would play her oldie but goodies as she listened to us. Sundays was the day that I would see her at her best, she was about family and family was about her.

It was now 1989 I was twenty-five years old and I was still very successful. It was as though everything I touched turned to gold. Money was still flowing in from the streets and the clubs. Because I was making so much money, I started to invest in myself. Purchasing different cars every few months had become an addiction I went from a BMW 325i to a Mercedes 190 to my summer car the Nissan 300zx then back to the Mercedes. I was also very generous with my ladies, depending on what they brought to the table I would bless them with luxurious gifts. One may be put up in a pen house the other may have received a BMW. It all depended on how I felt and how I wanted to see them, but like Willie always told me to do I stacked my money, so I had a nice nest egg saved up. Now that I was able to take care of Aunt Mary, every Sunday I would tell her that I wanted to do something special for her the main thing was moving her out of Harlem. She would brush it off curse me out in a playful way and tell me that she didn't want anything. It uses to bother me because if anyone deserved it, it was her.

Our Sunday's came around quickly there was a particular Sunday that I went to visit her with some chick I was seeing, the minute I walked through the door she yelled out from the kitchen "Is that Janine" I told her no and introduced her to this girl as my girlfriend she suddenly came storming at her and asked again "Are you Janine?" My girl was respectful about the question and answered, "No ma'am."

"Well then you need to get the fuck out of my house you fucking whore!" I was shocked, yet not surprised. I chucked it up to her being drunk. Homer came over to me later on in the day and told me that she had been acting real erratic lately. Yeah, she would spazzed out on people all the time when drinking but there was something different in how she was behaving. She was supposedly coming in and out of scenarios in her head she was also becoming forgetful and confused, which was affecting her daily functions. He was concern that something might seriously be wrong with her, but what did I know, so I didn't take it seriously. If I would have known then what I know now I would have recognized the signs of dementia. Aunt Mary was getting worst by the day and I still didn't see it, until I decided to go over to the house to check on her one day.

When I walked into the house, I found her sitting on the new sofa I had bought for her, yes, I made her go with me to a furniture store on 125th St. to pick out a new living room set. Although she didn't want anything from me, I insisted that she pick out the most expensive set in the showroom. Any way she was complaining that her leg was hurting her. She massaged it with her skinny fragile hands it in hopes of getting some type of relief. Aunt Mary continually asked for Epsom salt to soak her feet I noticed the tears in her eyes I scooped her up and commence to take her to the hospital. She wrapped her arms around my neck and started to say

"My son is so strong I love you my son." You have no idea what that did to me. I waited years to hear those words. Aunt Mary was my everything and to hear that no matter how many times she insulted me while growing up she really did love me.

I rushed her to the hospital took her through the emergency room where they examined her and decided to admit her. In my heart I felt that she was okay and that I could go handle my business. I had to go back home to South Carolina where my new wife Starr was waiting for me. When I got a call from Homer telling me that I had to come home. That call put the fear of God in me I rushed back to New York to find that the doctors had amputated her leg. When I walked into the hospital room Aunt Mary looked up at me with a blank look in her eyes. She looked so frail, sad and devastated.

Homer was sitting by her side, that's one thing Homer loved her took care of her and protected her this is why I couldn't understand why he consented to the removal of her leg without getting a second opinion. The doctors diagnosed her with a really bad infection called cellulitis. They said that the infection had spread throughout her whole leg causing blood poisoning and the best thing to do was to amputate. Homer agreed without hesitation. Aunt Mary was so confused, I could see that she was hurt and because of that her immune system became compromised. Aunt Mary passed away a few days later.

I was broken hearted for more reasons than one. My aunt my mom the woman who took me in, cared for me as a child, built up my strength and saved my life was now gone.

What really fucked me up was that no matter how much money I had. I wasn't able to save my MOTHER in return.

That year was one of the roughest years of my life not only did I lose Aunt Mary I also lost Sam Jr. my pops.

After Aunt Mary's funeral I got back on the road to go home, South Carolina. That trip took forever, my heart felt like it was on fire tears flowed from my eyes every few miles as I thought about my upbringing in Harlem and all that I had went through. I was ready for a change that's why I had decided to leave the apartment in Hackensack N.J. marry

Starr and buy that mansion. That level of success was made to either make you grow as a man or take you down like the great FUCKING titanic. I was blessed to have some wise men in my life to guide me.

When I reached my destination, I pulled up to the drive way stopped my car and stared at my house it was so big that I could have moved aunt Mary and Homer into it and still have room. What was the point in accomplishing so much if you didn't have the people you loved to share it with, I felt empty.

Death had never been the topic of conversation for me, sure I have discussed varies deaths where people have lost their lives to the lifestyle people got killed all the time in the hood because we envisioned a different life. A better one but in our world, it was all about survival.

Aunt Mary's sudden death was personal it touched home. In life we take things for granted, we imagine the people that we love are going to live forever. Harlem would never be the same Sundays would never be the same Mother's Day well I had to learn how to celebrate all of the mothers that helped raise me because the only mother I knew passed away two days before Mother's day. As I think back about that time in my life, I realize that I was in a deep depression. I went from feeling content and accomplished to feeling guilty. The thought of not being able to help my aunt affected me in the worst way. I stayed in South Carolina grieving thinking and hoping that the overwhelming feeling of losing her would pass.

It was now August of 1989 three months after Aunt Mary's Death that I got a phone call from my grandmother telling me that I needed to come home because my father Sam Jr. had died. I remember Starr staring at me as though to say, not again. She was so supportive of me while I dealt with my grief and I appreciated her but I was very distant towards her, towards life towards anything that had meaning. It takes a strong woman to love and support a man that dwelled in guilt. When I saw how she looked at me I suddenly began to feel better I suddenly became stronger. I wasn't about to let us down we had plans and nothing was going to stop us from perusing them

I jumped back on the highway and drove back to Harlem this time I was angry, bitter and full of rage. Again, I didn't understand why my family didn't take me up on my invitation to come live with me. I had so much space and I wanted them to live differently but their addictions kept them there.

The day that I closed on my mansion I spoke with my pops and told him to come with me to South Carolina I told him that he didn't have to live the way that he was living. He was drinking more than usual and it didn't help that his woman was drinking too. I told him that it was time to move away that he would have his own room, shit I told him that he could have his own fucking wing if he wanted to. I knew that he was having a lot of problems with his woman, I also knew that her sons had a problem with him. Even if their mother created some of the problems her sons were her sons and you already could imagine the rest. My father never told me anything about them fucking with him and they never told me anything about how my pops fought with their moms, but I knew, because I knew him, now here I was driving back to Harlem to bury him.

When I rolled up on 111th St on Manhattan Ave I got out of the car and walked over to the residential gates with the spikes on top. I noticed the rough edges where the police sawed off a section of it. That must have been where my father landed. My pops died in a horrific way, supposedly he was on the balcony smoking a cigarette when he fell on top of the spikes where his body stayed for about three hours until medical examiners showed up. I say supposedly because I didn't believe that story. I gazed up at the balcony and there was no way that he could have fallen on his own. To me my pops was pushed to his death once again I felt helpless. To know that he was living in a fucked-up situation was out of my control but what was in my control was vengeance. I had blood in my eyes I jumped back in the car and drove over to my grandmother's house and told her about my theory. My suspicion was that one of his woman's sons had pushed him off that balcony, there was but so much a nigga could take when seeing their mother being abused although she was abusive too.

My grandmother was very upset that I planned on calling on peoples and going back to confront them, I was zoned out.

She started to cry asking me not to do anything, she had expressed that Sam Jr. was her son and if she wasn't going to peruse an investigation that I shouldn't do anything either. She went on to tell me that she had loss too many family members already and that she didn't want to lose me.

First my grandfather Sam Sr. in 1988, then Aunt Mary earlier that year and now her son Sam Jr. She was the voice of reason and her reasoning made me calm down. I wasn't there to give her any grief she was up in age and I didn't want to be the cause any more heartache.

After Sam Jr. funeral I drove back to South Carolina my body was exhausted my heart was broken and my mind was not right.

Sam Jr. died on August 3rd I made it back home on the 6th and on the 9th I received another phone call. This time it was Tanya who called my house telling my wife that she needed to talk to me because she was in the hospital getting ready to give birth. Starr knew that Tanya was pregnant it was no secret I was always straight up and honest with Starr and she really didn't care because she was the WIFE. Let me remind you that Tanya was the first one that I called and asked to move with me to South Carolina and she said no.

What I didn't tell you is why she said no, Tanya told me that she couldn't come with me because she had to go with her sister Twana to Colombia to bury her baby father who had just been killed. Due to me explaining to her why I wanted to leave New York her response to me was in no way shape or form acceptable to me.

My response to her was that he was already dead and was she really going to choose her sister over me. I needed her, I needed to get out of the city, and I needed a change. When she turned her back on me, I walked away without a fight and married Starr. I had options and that is why people shouldn't put all of their eggs in one basket. Everyone wants to be number one, but they don't want the responsibility that comes with being Number one. Tanya was already pregnant when I picked up and left but I gave her the first right of refusal everything and everyone in my life served a purpose her purpose had come to an end when she said no to me.

Tanya called, Starr gave me the message but she didn't give me time to call her back the phone rang again this time was Twana screaming and hollering about why I wasn't at the hospital. The conversation went from me trying to tell her that I was not in Harlem to her disrespecting me and my wife. I was already going through enough I really didn't need all that extra shit. They made it so bad that I disappeared on Tanya when I finally surfaced four months later, I contacted Tanya told her I was driving to the city to meet my son. The plan was for me to pick her up then drive to the stores so that I could buy Tyriq everything he needed. When I arrived at Lefrak City, I told her to come outside, by the time she got downstairs I was already walking to the passengers' seat. I asked her to drive because I was tired from driving all night when she came around to the front of the car, she noticed that the license plate read Starr Mercedes she got behind the wheel pulled out and commence to driving I leaned back in the seat and thought about my son I was excited about meeting him and finally being a part of his life. I noticed that she was driving faster than usually and she started to press her foot down on the gas. Tanya started to yell at me talking about how fucking dare you pull up in this bitch's car. Her tensions were to crush the car into a wall with me in it. I grabbed the wheel and screamed out stop the fucking car when she finally did, I put the car in park shut it down got out and went to the drives side and told her to get the fuck out. She got out made a scene crying screaming yelling accusing me of disrespecting her. I didn't see it that way she was the one who didn't want to come with me what was I supposed to do sit around and wait forever I refused to allow anyone to have something over my head so I moved on and moved out. The streets were on fire bodies dropping all over Harlem I had to get out the game or I was going to end up in prison or dead.

It was my time to start anew and I wasn't going to allow anyone to stand in the way, even in the alphabets I came before U. I had to take care of me before I could take care of anyone else. I left Tanya standing in the middle of road gave her some money for my son and I pulled off. I never spoke to her again and I never got to meet my son that day. In my line of work I couldn't afford to get caught up in someone else emotional rollercoaster I had plans and my kids were a part of it but their mothers used them against me even when I couldn't be there for one reason or another they made it seem as though if I wasn't in a relationship with them I couldn't be with my kids.

As I got older, I tried to make it right with my kids some were able to forgive me some weren't open to hearing me out. I just hope that with my words they can get a better understanding that I'm human and with all that I have been through I was a legend in the making, most importantly I got out the game alive.

There was no returning back for the great Sammy O.

CHAPTER 29

YOU CAN'T HAVE THE COW
WITHOUT THE CALF

My past and everything that I have overcome was a
blessing. Some may see it as the road to damnation I
see it as the road to redemption. The streets raised me but I
saved me, by making the decision to walk away from the game
while I still had the chance. While I was still in one piece
mentally, spiritually and emotionally.

I walked away I got married to my beautiful wife Monique,
moved out to ATL with my three kids Ashley, Samson, Samara
and my dog Blue. And made a life for myself.

Looking out onto my home sometimes I can't believe that
I'm here and everything that it took to get here at one point
felt impossible. Lord knows the road was not easy, I went
through some shit but gods plan was for me to live life like I
was meant to live, on my terms.

The game will always be there, I know this from experience,
so many times I have walked away from the lifestyle only to

find myself being drawn right back to it. However, my wife and kids always put things right back into prospective for me. It takes a real man to share his story from a different point of view. It takes courage to share what made me attracted to the glitz and glamour and it takes discipline to know when to walk away.

I'm sure that everyone thought this book was going to be based on the who is who and who did what. Nah this story was written for the kid who was not supposed to make it but did.

To the next generation of hustlers, I will not tell you not to go out on the street, however if you make the decision to do so. You have to be prepared for what comes with the streets. Death, incarceration, or addiction DO NOT set yourself up for a downfall. The game is not for everyone and everyone is not cut out for the game. I was one of the lucky ones!

The End

Dear Harlem

Everything I am, Everything I have and Everyone I know I owe to you. You've been my home since I was a child and no matter where I may reside, I always come back to you. Growing up I always knew I lived in the greatest forty-five-block radiuses in the world. I've learned so much from you, from my street smarts to my communication and negotiation skills. People can recognize a Harlemite from anywhere from the way we walk to the way we talk; our swag is different and when asked where are you from I am always proud to say Harlem.

You inspired me to dream big, you showed me how to move with the times to grow to learn to appreciate even the little things. I'm more the grateful for all of your lessons. You were and will always be my favorite experience.

I thrived in your community, I've watched you transition from the abandoned buildings the drug infested streets and the violence endured by those who didn't know how to live a healthy life to high risers and sidewalk café but with all of those changes your roots will never change.

I didn't choose you Harlem you choose me no matter what I went through you always protected me in some way, if I was hungry you feed me if I was out on the streets with nowhere to sleep you would always guide me towards safety.

My family chose to raise me in your hood and I saw that their parenting skills weren't all that good not because they didn't want to be a positive example for me, they were just caught up in the reflection of the what Harlem use to be, the environment in which I lived in was not that great but you stepped in to protect me, always.

You assured me that no matter what I am going through your music, your aroma and your people would look out for me. As an adult when I was going through relationship problems instead of apologizing to my people, I would ride around your streets with my top down blasting music, while thinking about the dumb shit I've done.

No matter what our streets are going through you know how to bring our people together, from the annual Father's Day cookout on Morningside drive to Harlem Week, we came out to represent and there is nothing like it. It's a feeling only people from Harlem would understand and that's what I love about you, it's indescribable and I see why people gravitate to Harlem and never leave.

With my greatest appreciation I am honored to be one of your sons.

Love Sammy O

Aunt Mary and Sammy O

Sammy O South Carolina

Sammy O the Brother Hood

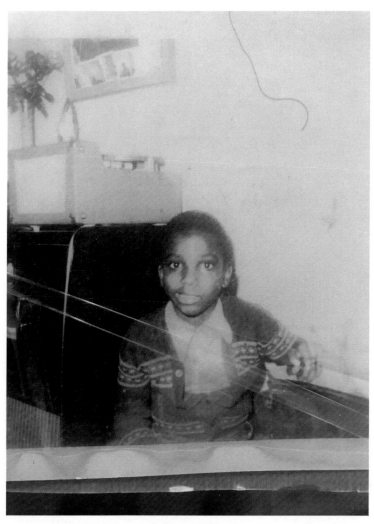

Sammy O

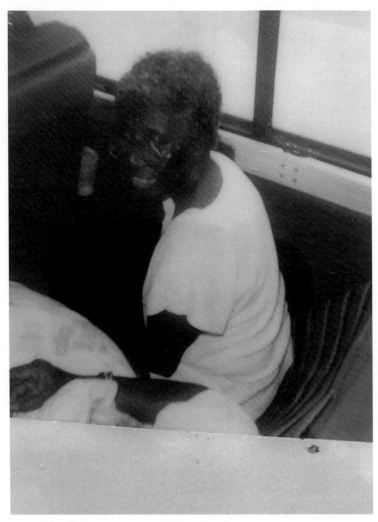

Aunt Mary

My Mother Beverly Harris

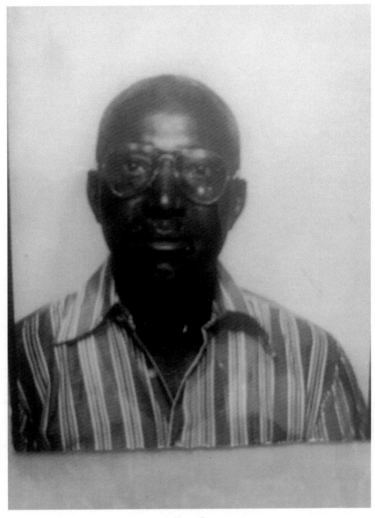

Sam Sr

Sammy O & Willie Burgers

Sammy O & Slim

Sammy O

Big AL 117th & Sammy O & Eric

Sammy O & Bizz

Sammy O Hot Rod Ty Pat Porter

Sammy O & Damion

Sammy O & Timbo

DFerg & Sammy O

Sammy O & Sheila

Sammy O

Sammy O & Samara

Sammy O & Spencer

Sammy O & Friends

Sammy O & Noreaga

Sammy O & Duces

Author Sexy & Sammy O

Sammy O Red r.i.p. Rick Dog

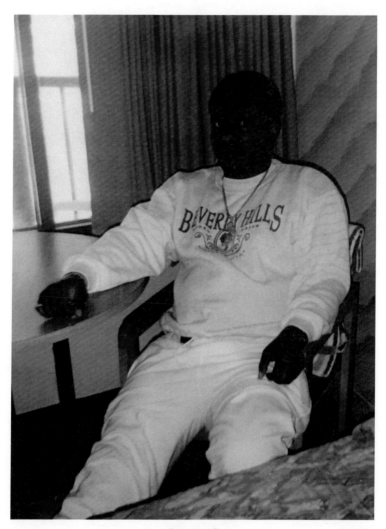

Sammy O

Nyesha Sammy O Keasha Sheila Bob

Sammy O & Quarterfield

Wise Timbo Sammy O Ty

Sammy O & T.Ferg

Sammy O & Guy Woods

Metal Sammy O Rob Gunn D.Boss

RIP Skeeta

Bro Kim Sammy O Wayneo

Samson Sammy O

111th st brotherhood

D.Ferg, Rick Dog, Mike Cock, Black Rodney, Troy

Sammy O - Baby Bob

Tu - Sammy O - Hotrod - Janice

Sammy O - Tony Dread - RIP JB

Sammy O and Nate

Sammy O & Daughter Shelby

Daugher Monay

Alicia-SammyO-Shelby-Tyriq-Samson

Bear -Sammy O

Jumbo-MikeBooth-SammyO

Wendy - Sammy O - Deborah - Sophia

Grandma Ruby

Pop's Sam Brown Jr.

Lee AKA young Sammy O